Julia Harris May

Songs from the Woods of Maine

Julia Harris May

Songs from the Woods of Maine

ISBN/EAN: 9783337181833

Printed in Europe, USA, Canada, Australia, Japan

Cover: Foto ©Thomas Meinert / pixelio.de

More available books at **www.hansebooks.com**

SONGS

FROM THE

WOODS OF MAINE

BY

JULIA H. MAY

G. P. PUTNAM'S SONS

NEW YORK   LONDON
27 WEST TWENTY-THIRD STREET   24 BEDFORD STREET, STRAND

The Knickerbocker Press

1894

To My Sister

SARA RICE MAY

My own! though vanished from my eyes,
  I lift these woodland songs to you,
  Just as of old I used to do,
To "look them over" in the skies.

And though it be, alas! too late
  To hear your answer, every line
  That seems, indeed, half yours, half mine,
To you I dare to dedicate.

CONTENTS.

	PAGE
IF WE COULD KNOW	3
THE COMMON SONG	4
MY BEST	5
THE HAPPY HILLS OF STRONG	6
O! WANDERERS OF MAINE	9
THE OLD RED SCHOOLHOUSE	11
A LEAF FOR WHITTIER'S GRAVE	14
BOTH	15
TRANSFORMATION	16
SOME DAY	18
THE WINDS OF MEMORY	20
CHANGED	21
HER MEMORY	23
THE SANDY RIVER	24
WHEN BUDS BEGIN TO BLOW	24
DREAMING	25
OUR HOME	27
WHICH ONE?	28
BEYOND THE PINES	29
ARE THEY GLAD?	30
BACK AGAIN	31
IF WE MIGHT	32
IMMORTALITY	34
MYSTERIES	35

JOYS TO COME	37
GONE	38
A SUMMER SONG	40
WHEN APRIL SHOWERS COME DOWN	41
DISCIPLINE	43
HOME AGAIN	45
BELIEF	45
BEAT QUICK, MY HEART	46
THE PASSING OF TENNYSON	48
WHEN LEAVES ARE LYING LOW	49
THY WILL BE DONE	50
IN PART	51
MY PORTION	53
HER BIRTHDAY	54
OCTOBER	55
A WINTER LULLABY	56
HOMEWARD	57
FREE	58
OH, FOR THE HILLS AGAIN!	61
GOING ABROAD	62
SURE	63
THE AUTUMN MIRACLE	64
AN ORIENTAL WISH	64
A WINTER FANCY	65
IF I KNEW WHERE	66
WAIT	68
LOWLAND MUSIC	69
OUTSIDE	70
DIVIDED	71
A BROKEN DREAM	72
MARY LYON	73
THOUGHT'S TRYST	74
AT WORK	76
AT REST	77
LOST—MY BOY	78
TRANSPLANTED	80

Contents.

	PAGE
LOVING ECHOES	81
A STAR CAN BE AS PERFECT AS A SUN	83
THE HAPPY CHOICE	84
SAYS I AND SAYS HE	86
A WEDDING SONG	89
MOTHER'S GIRL	90
WHEN MERRY SLEIGH BELLS RING	91
WINTER VIOLETS	93
LIVING STILL	94
THAT BLESSED SPRING	94
OH, SUMMER SKY!	95
LIFE	96
A RONDEAU—THE CHILD AND THE RIVULET	97

SONNETS.

TRUST	101
POSSESSION	102
SING AND LOOK UP	102
RECOGNITION	103
THE OLD PETITION	104
SUCCESS	104
OPPORTUNITY	105
THE OLD CLOCK	106
THE AWAKING	106
A NEW-YEAR'S SONNET	107
OUT-DOOR MUSIC	108
THROUGH TRUST	108
FROM PAGE TO PAGE	109
LIFTED	110
TO J. E. S	110
UNCERTAINTY	111
SEAWARD	112
AURORA	112
UNSATISFIED	113

PERSONAL POEMS.

FOR MY FRIENDS.

	PAGE
GRANDMOTHER'S FLOWER	117
FOURTEEN HAPPY YEARS	119
MY NEW-YEAR'S WISH	121
HIS BIRTHDAY	122
"GOD KNOWS WHY"	124
FOUR YEARS AGO	125
"BE BRAVE"	126
ONE YEAR AGO	127
YOU WOULD NOT WISH HER BACK	129
HANGING THE PICTURES	130
TILL DEATH DO PART	131
FULFILMENT	132
MEMORY'S CLASS	133
OH, NO! NOT OLD	137

MISCELLANEOUS.

I

MISCELLANEOUS

IF WE COULD KNOW.

IF we could know
  Which of us, darling, would be first to go,
Which would be first to breast the swelling tide,
And step alone upon the other side.

If it were you,
Should I walk softly, keeping death in view?
Should I my love to you more oft express,
Or should I grieve you, darling, any less—
If it were you?

If it were I,
Should I improve the moments slipping by?
Should I more closely follow God's great plan,
Be filled with sweeter charity to man—
If it were I?

If we could know;
We cannot, darling; and, 't is better so.
I should forget, just as I do to-day,
And walk along the same old stumbling way—
If I could know.

I would not know
Which of us, darling, will be first to go.
I only wish the space may not be long
Between the parting and the greeting song;
But when, or where, or how we 're called to go,
I would not know.

THE COMMON SONG.

IF it is never mine
    To be a brilliant star;
  Shall I, for shame, refuse to shine,
    Nor send one beam afar?
The smallest star its perfect work hath done
If it hath twinkled—
        Let me then be one.

  If it is never mine
    To be a mighty river,
  A rushing Rhone, a castled Rhine,
    Shall I lie still forever?
A little brook beside a rose can run,
And make it blossom—
        Let me then be one.

My Best.

If it is never mine
   To sing a lofty song,
  Shall I blot every lowly line
   And tuneless move along?
The common song the common folk hath won
And soothed their sorrows—
              Let me then sing one.

MY BEST.

I MAY perform no deed of great renown,
   No glorious act to millions manifest,
Yet, in my little labors up and down,
      I do my best.

I may not paint a perfect masterpiece,
   Nor carve a statue by the world confest
A miracle of art; yet, will not cease
      To do my best.

My name is not upon the rolls of fame,
   'T is on the page of common life imprest;
But I keep marking, marking just the same,
      And do my best.

Sometimes I sing a very simple song,
   And send it outward, to the east or west;
Although in silentness it rolls along,
      I do my best.

Sometimes I write a very little hymn,
   The joy within me cannot be represt ;
Though no one reads, the letters are so dim,
      I do my best.

And if I see some fellow-traveller rise
   Far, far above me, still, with quiet breast,
I keep on climbing, climbing toward the skies,
      And do my best.

My very best, and if, at close of day,
   Worn out, I sit me down awhile to rest,
I still will mend my garments, if I may,
      And do my best.

It may not be the beautiful or grand,
   But I must try to be so careful, lest
I fail to do what 's put into my hand,
      My very best.

Better and better every stitch must be,
   The last a little stronger than the rest,
Good Master, help mine eyes, that they may see
      To do my best.

THE HAPPY HILLS OF STRONG.

O ! HILLS of Strong ! my native hills !
   Wherever I may be,
The thought of you forever fills
   The depths of memory.

I long to stand upon your slope
   When right seems merged in wrong,
And bury doubt and lift up hope
   Above the Hills of Strong!

I wander far, I cross the sea,
   I visit foreign lands;
Above the shrines of Italy
   I lift my wondering hands;
I mount the Alps; I pass the Rhine;
   But ever look along
The far horizon's western line
   That hides the Hills of Strong!

I climb the summits of the East,
   Vesuvius I scale;
On ruins of the past I feast
   In Andalusia's vale;
I cross the lakes of Switzerland,
   I hear the Highland song;
But still come blowing o'er the strand
   Your breezes, Hills of Strong!

I roam across the continent,
   And climb the peaks between
The east and west; my eyes are bent
   To look for hills unseen.
The heights are grand, the depths are vast;
   But there is something wrong;
And so to you I turn at last,
   My happy Hills of Strong!

I seem to hear " The Sandy " wind
   Among the rocks ; I see
A home ; inside its doors, I find
   Remembered melody.
I walk the bridge that spans the stream,
   Where swaying mem'ries throng,
Until I waken from a dream,
   Upon the Hills of Strong !

My happy hills ! your rocks have felt
   The presence of her feet,
Who once beside my fireside knelt,
   And whispered, " Love is sweet."
I call her name ; the rocks reply,
   The woods the sound prolong ;
I almost hear her passing by,
   Upon the Hills of Strong !

Oh ! when I cross the bridge of death,
   And meet the feet that wait
To walk with mine, may my last breath
   (Lord, let it not be late !)
Be drawn within my native vale,
   And may I look along
Your tops, until my sight shall fail,
   My dear old Hills of Strong !

O! WANDERERS OF MAINE!

O! Wanderers from the land of Maine! the
 perfume of the pine
Is mingled with your memory—Her violet vales
 entwine
Memorial wreaths—She calls for you—O! must
 she call in vain?
Come back, your mother longs for you, O! Wanderers of Maine!

From mountain heights your feet have climbed,
 from Abraham and Blue,
She looks across the continent and strains her eyes
 for you.
Above the prairies of the West, she calls and calls
 again:
"Come back, my children! Come to me, O!
 Wanderers of Maine!

"My hills are high, but from their tops the sky-fed
 waters run.
My snows are deep and soft and white, and warm
 my summer sun,
My springs are like the crystal clear, my clouds are
 full of rain,
Come back from yonder sun-burnt sands, O!
 Wanderers of Maine!"

Come back! The peaks will welcome you; the
    valleys laugh with joy,
The snow-flakes leap to touch your hands as when
    you were a boy,
The cow-bells' music, faint and sweet, is tinkling
    down the lane,
To meet your footsteps coming back, O! Wan-
    derer of Maine!

Come back! There's room enough! O! hear the
    voice of Kennebec!
The ocean calls. She looks for you on every
    home-bound deck.
The Androscoggin murmurs, "Come." Aroos-
    took's fertile plain
Is beckoning her Wanderers to the motherland of
    Maine.

Come back! Come back! Though ye might stay
    but for a little while,
And give your mother yet once more the gladness
    of your smile;
For she will clasp you in her arms and beg you to
    remain
Beneath the perfume of the pines, O! Wanderer of
    Maine!

"Come back!" she cries. Alas! to-night, along
    the west-winds' swell
A bell's deep tone is echoing—"O! mother Maine,
    farewell!"

The weary wanderer lieth low. He cannot come
  again
To rest among the apple-blooms beneath the skies
  of Maine.

The west winds whisper many a name to home-
  folks strangely sweet,
"O! Casco-cradled Longfellow!" the surf-bound
  billows beat.
"O! doers of heroic deeds! O! land-lamented
  Blaine!
O! humbler souls of holy life, lost Wanderers of
  Maine!"

*   *   *   *   *   *   *   *   *

Dear Wanderers, who wander yet! if we no more
  may meet
Until the Land of the Beyond shall press your
  weary feet;
We still will lift our banner high, and sing the old
  refrain,
For ye are ours for evermore! O! Wanderers of
  Maine!

THE OLD RED SCHOOLHOUSE.

I REMEMBER the old red schoolhouse,
  On the other side of the stream;
Where we went to school together, Will,
  When life was like a dream.

Where we played " high spy " or " touch the
    gool "
  With Ben and James and Lou ;
And jumped the rope of joy and hope,
  Do you remember too ?

I went to the dear old schoolhouse,
  Only the other day.
And I sat on the slope, where we jumped the
    rope,
  But I did not care to stay.
The blinds were closed ; the glass was gone ;
  And, would you believe it, Will !
They were turning round, where our wits were
    ground,
  The wheels of a cider mill.

I sat on the slope, where we jumped the rope,
  But I did not want to stay.
My thoughts went back on a well worn track,
  And I went to school that day.
Old Grimes was there. His bushy hair
  Stood up, and his piercing eyes
Gazed down on me from the used to be,
  With a sort of dazed surprise.

Then I seemed to stand with an eager band,
  For a while, in the spelling class.
They were choosing me ; I was proud, may be,
  To be doing so well, but alas !

I had finished "boquet" and "phthisic" and "dey"
   And "business" and "anodyne,"
When I failed, and Will (he is doing it still)
   Took the place that was higher than mine.

Then I seemed to be walking the sloping aisle
   Till I sat on the low front seat,
With Addie and Nancy and Susan and Em,
   To feel for a little heat.
We were "reading in concert" now soft and low,
   Now soaring at highest pitch,
"Charge, Chester, charge! On, Stanley, on!"
   At the wave of the master's switch.

Ah! we have been "charging on," Will!
   Since then, in the battle of life;
And some have gone down, where the grasses brown
   Have hidden the field of strife.
And only a few of the band are left,
   Addie and Nancy and Phil,
And you and I, to talk of our youth,
   And the schoolhouse under the hill.

You have your treasures in earth and heaven.
   And mine, they are all on high,
But we both have a beautiful work to do
   For the feet that are passing by.
For the steps that tire; then higher, higher,
   Let us climb, old schoolmate, till
We reach the top, and our burdens drop,
   On the other side of the hill.

A LEAF FOR WHITTIER'S GRAVE.

ONE leaf upon thy grave I 'd throw,
    My poet sweet and true,—
One leaflet that unseen may go
    To fade beneath the dew.

O singer, sweet, and true, and grand !
    In heaven, dost thou care
That aching hearts, through all the land,
    Send up the silent prayer

Which thou hast taught them ? Dost thou know
    How hands that never grasped
Thine own with sympathetic glow,
    Together have been clasped,

Because of thine ? If thou dost know
    How lips have longed to speak
Their gratitude ; what blessings flow
    From tongues that vainly seek

To tell thy greatness, then, O ! let
    This thought thy glory be :
That souls have climbed from Olivet
    To heaven, upheld by thee.

BOTH.

Both of us, dear,
    Yes, both
The last soft rustling of these elms shall hear,
And then shall go
To sit beneath the Tree of Life ; and so
Why should we fret
That one, the leaves of healing first, will get?

Both of us, dear,
Yes, both
Shall, for the last time, see the ripples clear
Of yonder brook,
And then, upon the living waters look ;
Why should it seem
So hard to wait an hour beside the stream?

Both of us, dear,
Yes, both
The pearly gates shall some glad hour draw near,
And enter in,
Freed from this load of suffering and sin ;
How blest we are,
If one, going first, can hold the gates ajar!

Both of us, dear,
Yes, both
Shall see the last faint twilight disappear,

Or moon, or star,
From this low window where our clasped hands
    are ;
Why feel dismay,
If I, for you, should seek the upward way?

Both of us, dear,
Yes, both
Shall learn the final lesson of a year,
And then shall rise
To the Great Master teaching in the skies ;
Is it not meet
That one go first to find the other's seat?

Both of us, darling!
Both ;
Then why so loth
That a few years apart our steps should be?
Years are but minutes to eternity.

TRANSFORMATION.

Out of the sky of the Long Ago
    There falls on my heart to-day,
A snatch of song I used to know,
    An olden roundelay,
And the mystery of joy and grief
    Its hidden meaning knows,
The crimson flush of the autumn leaf
    Is the blush of the summer rose.

Transformation.

The robins are singing above my head,
    And the buttercups shine at my side ;
The east is so blue, and the west is so red,
    And the summer world is so wide.
And I say to myself : " O, the June is so brief ! "
    But I hear, as the river flows :
" The crimson flush of the autumn leaf
    Is the thought of the summer rose."

The mountains are blue and clear to-day,
    And to-morrow, perchance, will be ;
But the apple-blossoms have dropped away,
    And the coming fruit I see.
And over it all the sunlight glows,
    And the seed foretells the sheaf,
As the tender blush of the summer rose
    Is the flush of the autumn leaf.

The elm-trees bend to the evening breeze,
    And the clover scents the air ;
And the brook ripples on behind the trees,
    And the valleys are green and fair ;
And I hold to my heart the sweet belief,
    If the east wind rudely blows,
That the crimson flush of the autumn leaf
    Is the blush of the summer rose.

The children are glad, as their tripping feet
    Come home from the noon-tide play,
And the mothers kiss them with smiles as sweet
    And with voices as merry as they.

But into the little heart a grief,
   As into the old heart grows,
And the crimson flush of the autumn leaf
   Is the blush of the summer rose.

The clouds are as red in the evening sky,
   As the clouds of the eastern morn,
And the rose-bud on that bush close by,
   Like the full-blown rose, has a thorn.
And for ever and aye to the rivers rush,
   This melody comes and goes,
Of the autumn leaf, the crimson flush,
   Is the blush of the summer rose.

The myrtle bloom, in the graveyard lot,
   Is as blue as the garden flower,
And the sorrow of each neglected spot
   Remembers its joyful hour.
And the prayer of earth is the praise of heaven,
   And time will its meaning disclose,
As the crimson flush of the autumn leaf
   Is the blush of the summer rose.

SOME DAY.

SOME day,
   The last June roses I shall pick, and stay
To see the mountain shadows and the blue
Of the soft summer sky, my last with you.
Will any change in leaf, or hill, or sky
Tell us an angel draweth nigh?

Some Day.

Some day,
I shall my head upon my pillow lay,
Never to lift it up until I rise,
Within my mansion ready in the skies ;
Will your soft touch, or tear, or silent prayer,
Be with me there ?

Some day,
I shall go through a pearly gate, and stray
Along the margin of a crystal sea,
For the first time, and learn its mystery ;
Whose clasping hand for mine will throbbing wait ?
And who will lead me through the swinging gate ?

Some day,
Perchance, I may unto the angels say,
What are they doing ? Who are shedding tears
Because I 've spilled my little cup of years ?
Or who are happy as they used to be,
Forgetting me ?

Some day,
I think I shall not backward look, for they
Who are redeemed are glad, and even there,
For your dear love I know that I shall care,
And if I could, in Heaven, your sorrow see,
Would it be Heaven to me ?

Some day,
When, where, how long, oh, who would wish to
    say !

For the last time, our eyes shall fill with tears ;
We shall begin the bliss of endless years,
That day.

THE WINDS OF MEMORY.

UPON the western shore, to-night, I 'm sitting,—
    The shore that slopes to touch a boundless
  sea,—
And watch the white ships, inward, outward, flitting,
    And wonder when my ship will come for me ;
And where it lies, and whither it is going,—
I only hear the winds of memory blowing.

Across the cliffs of yesterday they 're coming,
    They fan my forehead with the forest air ;
Remembered melodies the hills are humming,
    A scent of pine-trees hovers everywhere ;
I hear again the bank-side brooklet flowing,
While all the winds of memory are blowing.

Blow on, sweet winds, your singing or your sighing
    Brings back to-night a half-forgotten tune.
Beneath the apple-blooms once more I 'm lying ;
    I feel the breath of girlhood's happy June ;
Life's early dawn, again I see it glowing,
While all the winds of memory are blowing.

A summer song, now faint, now fuller growing ;
   A far-off lullaby from mother lips ;
Love, living love, receiving and bestowing,
   I listen, listen, oh ! ye white-winged ships ;
I do not heed your coming or your going,
While all the winds of memory are blowing.

Upon the western shore, to-night, I'm sitting,—
   The shore that slopes to touch a boundless sea,—
And watch the billows upward, downward, flitting,
   But do not care how near the tide may be,
Or, if its waters touch my feet, not knowing,
While I can hear the winds of memory blowing.

CHANGED.

DEAR faded eyes !
   Ye were so full of tears for others' sighs ;
So full of smiles,
To cheer the pathway of the weary miles ;
So full of care,
When there was need or danger anywhere ;
Ye could not idly brook
One loveless look.

Dear pallid lips !
From out your paleness, now, no blessing slips ;
Once ye were red,
As yonder rose in yonder garden bed ;

Once ye would open
Only to let the gentle word be spoken;
How could we let you miss
One answering kiss?

Dear helpless feet!
Once ye were strong and firm and sure and fleet;
Ready to run
On any errand for sweet mercy done;
Ready to bear
The heavy end of every load of care;
How could we,
Your failing footstep e'er unnoticed, see?

Dear withered hands!
Ye were so eager to do love's commands;
So skilled to hold
The cup of blessing; tenderly enfold,
In your embrace,
The weary form, or cool the burning face;
How could we grasp
Some other hand, forgetful of your clasp?

Eyes! look not so;
Give me one glimpse of reason, ere you go.
Open, white lips!
And give one tender word in Death's eclipse.
Before those feet
Shall walk unfailingly the golden street,
Oh, let us see
Those eyes and lips just as they used to be!

HER MEMORY.

I CANNOT hear my mother's voice,
   I cannot see her face;
She nevermore will speak to me
   Within the dear old place.
The trees she loved, the cottage door,
Will feel her presence, nevermore.

Old Elms! Look down upon me now;
   Your boughs to-night are bare,
But summer time will give each one
   A foliage fresh and rare.
Yet she who loved your leaves to see,
Will watch no more the old elm tree.

Dear Stream, beyond the woodland bank!
   Your waters onward flow;
But nevermore her feet will haste
   Along your paths to go.
And nevermore she 'll walk with me,
And listen to your melody.

But, dear old Home! we 'll not forget
   The smiling of her face,
The heart shall listen for her step
   In each remembered place.
And these still empty rooms shall be
Filled up with her sweet memory.

THE SANDY RIVER.

A DROP from the summer rain-cloud,
    And a drop from the summer dew,
Kissing, and running together
    Far up the mountain blue.

A tiny spring on the hillside,
    Stealing down to a tiny lake,
And crooning the quiet murmur
    That baby brooklets make.

A thread of silver water
    Strung round the rocky hill,
Twisting in with another,
    And curving onward still.

A whisper of meadow lilies,
    A breath from the garden rose,
And down the smiling valley
    The Sandy river goes.

WHEN BUDS BEGIN TO BLOW.

WHEN buds begin to blow
    Where last year's leaflets lie,
When fields grow green, when violets show
    The color of the sky,
When fragrance fills the air,
    When twinkling stars can see

Shine up along the meadows bare
   The star-anemone :
O ! then the happy heart can sing
   To sleep its winter sorrowing ;
And joys spring up, and hopes mount high,
   When buds begin to blow.

When buds begin to blow
   And into blossoms spread,
My drooping hope learns how to grow,
   By these interpreted ;
Faith takes me by the hand
   That holds an opening flower,
And whispers, you will understand,
   In some swift coming hour,
How joy puts on a brighter bloom,
   That springs from sorrow, how the tomb
May be like yonder garden bed
   Where buds begin to blow.

DREAMING.

I KNOW a quiet place
   Beside a singing brook,
A study, hung with leafy lace,
   Where I can read my book,
And, as I turn its leaves, upon
   God's open volume look.
Below my rustic seat
   The bank descends a space,

Where stones run down, the brook to meet,
    And pat the water's face;
While, through the trees, across the brook,
    God's mountains I can trace.

Above my head, the pines
    Stretch to the bending sky;
And branch with clinging branch entwines
    Toward that blue vault, on high,
Where God's own wingèd songsters make
    Fresh music as they fly.

My happy song I sing;
    The brook sings back to me;
The waving boughs keep echoing
    A music glad and free,
While all the woodland air is brimmed
    With living melody.

O! merry singing stream!
    O! joyous swinging bough!
Are ye as happy as ye seem?
    And can ye tell me how
I seem to sit within a dream
    And cannot waken now?

Still in my quiet place,
    Beside the running stream,
Where past and present interlace,
    I dream my little dream;
And sometimes think I am awake,
    And things are what they seem.

OUR HOME.

BELOVÈD! when we pass away
   From this familiar spot,
I wonder who will come and stay
   In the deserted cot!
Beneath these elm trees, who will stand,
   And think that home is sweet,
When we have gone into that land
   Where parted households meet?

Oh! who will walk beside the stream,
   Or sit beneath the pine,
To dream again life's little dream,
   When 't is not yours nor mine?
Will some one fell my favorite tree?
   Pull down the mossy wall?
The things so dear to you and me,
   Will they destroy them all?

Whose name will be on yonder door?
   Whose pictures deck the walls?
Whose feet press roughly on the floor
   Where your dear footstep falls?
And when the years to centuries swing,
   Till all we love are dead,
Will any echo backward bring
   The words that we have said?

I hope the brook, down there, will miss
    An old familiar tone,
When, in a happier home than this,
    We talk with all our own ;
For oh ! this little home is sweet,
    Each corner is so dear !
Can heaven without it be complete ?
    I would that heaven were here.

WHICH ONE?

ONE of us, dear,
        But one,
Will sit by a bed with a nameless fear,
And clasp a hand,
Growing cold as it feels for the spirit land ;
        Darling, which one ?

One of us, dear,
        But one,
Will stand by the other's coffin bier,
And look and weep,
While those marble lips strange silence keep ;
        Darling, which one ?

One of us, dear,
        But one,
By an open grave will drop a tear,
And homeward go,
The anguish of an unshared grief to know ;
        Darling, which one ?

One of us, darling, it must be—
It may be, you will slip from me;
My little life may first be done;
I 'm glad we do not know which one.

BEYOND THE PINES.

BEYOND the belt of pines
    That bounds my bit of ground,
The sunset west this evening shines,
    And spreads its colors round.
With rosy pink it gleams and gleams,
    Where gold with blue entwines;
A land of dreams
The picture seems,
    That hangs beyond the pines.

The boughs fling out their green
    Mementos of the spring,
And, dark upon the shining sheen,
    To rocking winds they swing.
The red horizon bends, and blends
    With wavy sun-tipped lines.
Day upward sends
Adieux, and lends
    New glory to the pines.

A stretch of billowy snow
    This side the piney bank;
The tiny driftlets break and blow
    Where summer blossoms sank,

And, from the boughs, the snow-flakes fall,
  Till sunset glow declines,
And, like a wall
Of shade, is all
  The picture of the pines.

ARE THEY GLAD?

IF she were here
  To take my hand, and ask: "What is it, dear?"
She would not see the wrinkles on my face,
Nor note the silver where the gold had place;
Upon my faded lip she'd leave a kiss,
And whisper "Darling"; and she would not miss
The vanished rose, or, if she did, would say:
"How you have ripened since I went away!"
The blemishes that others might despise,
Would still be beautiful, in mother's eyes.

If she were here,
She would not mind the changes; if a tear
Should fill my eye, I know that she would see,
And give sweet consolation unto me,
Yet, in her heart, some things would little heed,
Knowing how much their discipline I need.
And so, I think, though Heaven be not far,
And friends can see us even as we are,
They may be glad, like loving motherhood,
Because they know *how* all things work for good.

BACK AGAIN.

TO MY SISTER, ON HER RECOVERY FROM DANGEROUS ILLNESS.

BACK to my arms, my darling!
   Back from the river's brink
You have come; oh, let me clasp you!
   And know you did not sink!
Did you feel the chilly water,
   Did you see the angel's wings,
Ere you turned from the icy river
   Backward to earthly things?

Back to my arms my darling!
   Back from the river's brink
You have come, and I am waking
   From a dream. Oh, let me think!
Did I take your hand this morning?
   Did I press you to my heart?
Did I weep, and did they tell me
   That we, to-day must part?

Yes, but you 're back, my darling!
   Back, for you could not go;
Could not leave me here so lonely,
   And longing for you so.
For I sit, to-night, by your bedside,
   And I clasp your life-warm hand;
While I think new thoughts that need no words
   To make you understand.

Back to my arms, my darling!
   Back to my beating side
You have come, and just behind you
   I hear the rolling tide.
But we'll lift again life's burden,
   Clasping each other still,
And we'll cross some time to the other side,
   Together, if God will.

IF WE MIGHT.

IF we might, oh! if we might
   Turn back the wheels of time, my friend, to-night;
If to the vale of childhood we could go,
And climb again, from those warm depths below,
To this steep hillside; live, from day to day,
The past, just as we lived it once, oh! say,
Would you be glad to tread the pathway o'er—
The same old steps again, no less, no more?

If we might, yes, if we might
Turn back the whirling wheels, my friend, to-night,
And slowly wind, from youth to middle age,
The tangled road; if every blotted page
We could omit, and let the good remain;
In life's brief book, skip all the grief and pain,
Would you be willing, then, to live them o'er—
The backward years that can return no more?

If We Might.

"If I might, oh! if I might,
Perhaps I would, perhaps I should, to-night.
I am not wise—old friendships were so true,
Old loves so sweet and even if I knew
I must have all the sorrow, all the pain,
For love's dear sake I might go back again;
The thorny pathway, to my willing feet,
Would not be hard—I think it would be sweet."

But if the spring, ah! if the spring
Lead on to summer; if the autumn bring
The winter snow-flakes; if the joyous chime
Of wintry bells ring in the blossom time;
Why would you live again the same old year,
Knowing another spring will soon be here?
The dead May violets rather should you kiss
And say "Next year they will be sweet as this."

And if the life, ah! if the life
We live on earth, so full of restless strife,
So full of joyfulness, or blessed peace,
Is beautiful, why should you wish to cease
The onward journey? Do not wish again
To live life over, even without the pain,
For oh, my friend! when life's last sun is set,
The bright next day is heaven, do not forget.

IMMORTALITY.

If it were true
    This life were all, and if to-day we knew,
When looking in the marble face of death,
That which we missed was nothing but a breath,
And when we gently closed the glassy eye,
The end of all things was but this—to die!

If it were true
Death's river we should fearfully pass through,
And then, beyond the dark, mysterious gate,
Endless oblivion should forever wait;
If all the days of sorrow and distress
Must terminate in utter nothingness.

If it were true
That all the sweet things we have learned to do,
And all the friends it is our joy to see,
Would be no more to you, no more to me,
That " Dust to dust " would hear no glad " Arise,"
And heaven were nothing but the starry skies.

If it were true
I would not know it, dear, oh, say, would you?
Unto my heart the fancy I would fold,
That yet another life this life would hold,
And, on the tombstone of each sweet affection,
I still would write, " There is a resurrection."

It is not true—
There is another life, for me, for you,
I think, I feel, I know that it is so,
A life more perfect than the one we know.
Ah ! tell me not that we shall cease to be—
I feel the pulse of immortality.

MYSTERIES.

BETWEEN two mysteries I stand,
    The vast unfathomed skies,
And that unpenetrated land
    Which underneath me lies.

What is beyond that fadeless blue ?
    Beyond that trembling star ?
Is there a spot no eye can view,
    Where space's limits are ?

Is there a point where length must cease,
    And breadth extend no more,
Where magnitude cannot increase,
    And height and depth are o'er ?

Is there a place where length meets length
    In endless circling lines,
Where gravitation's waning strength
    To nothingness declines ?

My reason cannot grasp the thought;
   Imagination tries,
In vain, to solve the riddle taught
   In those mysterious skies.

I look from sky to mother earth,
   Put to her lip my ear,
And ask the secret of her birth,
   No answer do I hear.

I ask the violet of its blue,
   The snow-flake of its white;
The violet only whispers, "Dew,"
   The snow-flake murmurs, "Light."

I ask the orchard of its leaf,
   The meadow of its wheat;
The apple and the ripened sheaf
   Look up, and answer, "Eat."

I ask the rocks beneath my tread,
   Their shadow to explain;
I see far down their hidden bed,
   But unknown depths remain.

The fire within, how does it burn?
   I ask, and vainly try
Unnumbered theories to learn,
   But none will satisfy.

Between two mysteries I stand,
  The vast unfathomed sky,
And that unpenetrated land
  Where I so soon must lie.

What is the soul? what is the mind?
  What is the life within?
I ask, but no solution find;
  I end as I begin.
*   *   *   *   *
From mystery, I turn to fact;
  To known from the concealed.
I dream no more, I only act,
  For duty is revealed.

JOYS TO COME.

WHEN disappointments rise,
    Or racking pain upon my pillow lies,
I wipe my tears at every darting pain,
    And softly cry,
    As low I lie,
I 'm glad *this* pang can never come again.

When, in life's summer heaven,
A cloud makes black the twilight of the even,
Or breaks upon my soul the pelting rain,
    Still bowing low,
    I smile to know,
I shall not have to face *this* storm again.

But, when the storm is past,
The soul's blue sky no longer overcast,
When throbbing joy replaces bitter pain,
  Then do I cry,
   As hope mounts high,
The joy that comes *will surely come again!*

For, joy, it seems to me,
Is but a foretaste of what is to be;
And sorrow's heaviest state,
Only the struggling of the joys that wait;
And thus, though many a bitter pang remain,
  At each I'll cry,
   The end draws nigh,
And *this one* cannot hurt my heart again.

GONE.

SHE has gone—my life and my light;
 Under the clover she lies.
The sun is no more at morning bright,
Nor the moon of the evening skies;
The days are long and drear,
And the nights no sweetness bring;
The wearisome weeks are cold and dark,
For the year has lost its spring—
The year has lost its spring,
And the summer forgot its June,
And the harp of my heart,

In its sweetest part,
Is forever out of tune.

Ah! the sky has lost its blue,
And the stars their twinkling ray;
And the garden has lost its fragrant breath,
Since my rose was stolen away;
The sky has lost its blue,
And the woods their nightingale,
And my heart has lost a love so true,
That the springs of its river fail;
Yes, the river has lost its spring,
And the Summer forgot its June,
And the harp of my heart,
In its sweetest part,
Is forever out of tune.

The rainbow has left the sky;
The south winds do not blow;
A shadow is passing slowly by,
Wherever my footsteps go.
Sweet summer! I loved you once,
But the beauty of every thing,
And the glory and sweetness have passed away,
Since my year has lost its spring;
Yes, the year has lost its spring,
And the summer forgot its June,
And the harp of my heart,
In every part,
Is forever out of tune.

A SUMMER SONG.

"Move slow, sweet June! Sweet June, move slow,
And let the apple-blossoms blow
A little longer; let the sky
Bend backward, as the hours pass by.
My darling, look," she said, " and write
A song with this refrain to-night.
' Oh, stay, sweet June, thy flowery feet—
Thou art so sweet; thou art so sweet.'"

"Move slow, sweet June, sweet June, move slow,"
I sang, and watched the lilies blow,
And saw the dandelions shine
Upon a hand held close in mine.
"Oh, stay, until the robins sing
Once more," our hearts kept whispering.
"Stay, stay, sweet June, thy flowery feet—
Thou art so sweet; thou art so sweet."

Sweet June, dear June, no longer stay;
Alone I sing, to-day, to-day;
Oh, linger not! stop not to tell
The tale I used to love so well,
But hasten, June, for I would go
Where flowers immortal bud and blow.
Dear June, sweet June, no longer stay—
Thou art so sad, so sad, to-day.

And yet, dear June, dear June, and yet
Thou still art sweet. Do I forget
How many hearts are glad as mine
In other Junes? Oh, blot that line,
That verse, my hand. Let lovers sing
To-day; let children's voices ring
With joy; for them delay thy feet,
Sweet June—thou art so sweet, so sweet.

WHEN APRIL SHOWERS COME DOWN.

WHEN April showers come down
    From blossom-loving skies,
And, peeping through the grasses brown,
    Bid sleeping buds arise,
Unto the woods, so sweet, so sweet,
    Beyond the stifled town,
I turn my feet,
Old friends to meet,
    When April showers come down.

I lift the mossy stone,
    Arbutus leaves to touch,
And whisper to them all alone,
    "I love you, O! so much."
And for a bud I look, I look
    Beneath their shining crown,
In every nook,
By fence or brook,
    When April showers come down.

One pink anemone
  Is first my voice to heed;
She lifts her starry eyes to me,
  Their language I can read.
And O! the world is free, is free
  I care not for its frown;
Do raindrops see the change in me
  When April showers come down?

Unto the fields I go,
  I climb the brookside steep;
I sit where violets used to blow,
  And wish they would not sleep;
'Neath dripping boughs I stay, I stay,
  Still heedless of renown.
"Come just this way
  Till merry May,"
    I sing as showers come down.

Unto my work, at last,
  I walk with lagging feet;
For raindrops do not fall so fast,
  Their touch will not be sweet.
And at my task I sing, I sing,
  All moody cares to drown;
Sweet thoughts upspring
To blossoming,
  When April showers come down.

DISCIPLINE.

A WAYWARD scholar, to the school of pain,
        Long years ago,
My Father sent me, saying : " Child ! remain
        Until you know
The lesson that, in future, you will need
For you are very ignorant indeed."

At first, with many bitter tears and sighs,
        I conned my task.
" What good from all these problems can arise ? "
        Presumed to ask,
And blindly learned the lesson of the years,
Through eyes that were so dim with homesick tears.

Sometimes, unto my Father I would write
        And sadly say :
" I cannot keep the rules ; oh ! if I might
        Go home to-day,
Or to a better school—please let me go—
Whose lessons will be easier to know ! "

My Father pitied me, and often sent
        Sweet words of cheer,
Or told me what the tangled questions meant,
        In terms so clear
That, for a while, I liked the school of pain,
And all its discipline seemed wise and plain.

But then, sometimes, the teachers were so stern,
   Sometimes, so queer,
I did not understand, I could not learn,
   I would not hear
The tender words my Father said to me,
When He came down his wayward child to see.

Sometimes I tried the hardest things to do,
   An easier way
Than that appointed, for I thought I knew
   Better than they,
The teachers in this blessed school of pain ;
I always had to do the task again.

At length, I sat me down unto my work
   With earnest will.
" I 'll do it as they wish, I will not shirk,
   I will be still,"
I said ; " and, though I do not understand,
I will obey the very least command."

And soon, the discipline no more seemed stern,
   The lines grew plain,
I longed, each day, more precious truths to learn ;
   I felt no pain,
For pain was pleasure, work was sweetest rest,
Because my Father told me it was best.

At last, I learned to love the school of pain ;
   That very day,

My Father came to see His child again ;
    We went away,
The dear untroubled home life to begin,
So much the better for the discipline.

HOME AGAIN.

BACK to my own dear hills I come
    From grander heights ; my lips were dumb
On those far mountain tops, but now
My heart speaks out ; my soul knows how
To syllable its joy. Alone,
I walked through crowds, a speck unknown ;
I am myself with thee, my own.

Back to the friends of other years ;
Back to the smiles, perchance the tears ;
To humble walks, in valleys sweet,
Familiar paths beneath my feet ;
Back to the winds from pine-trees blown,
To seed that 's waiting to be sown ;
Back from the heights to thee, my own !

BELIEF.

BECAUSE I would,
    I climbed the sunny slopes of maidenhood,
Youth's pathway was so fair, so fresh, so free ;
So far, so high, life's hilltops looked to me,
I thought not of the future—did not care

To think about it—whether it were fair
Beyond the summit ; every moment, glad
To pick the buds around me ; for I had
No doubts, no fears, believed that God was good,
Believed in heaven and immortality,
Because I would.

Because I must,
I lean to-day upon my staff of trust ;
The hilltops are not far ; I soon shall see
The other side burst forth. It cannot be
That I have climbed so far, and all for nought.
Ah, no ! Some glorious glimpses I have caught,
And cannot help but take the downstretched hand,
And cling to it as tottering I stand.
Oh ! tell me not that I am empty dust ;
My spirit is—Belief ! I hold to thee,
Because I must.

BEAT QUICK, MY HEART.

BEAT quick, my heart !
    Still faster, faster, let the life depart !
The heart in unison with thee is still ;
The pulse that felt thy palpitating thrill
Can throb no longer ; eyes that once would weep
If thou shouldst stop thy beating, are asleep,
And from their folded lids no tears can start
To soothe thy sorrows. Oh, beat quick, my heart !

Beat Quick My Heart.

Hasten, my feet !
To walk the paths your future course must meet.
The step I loved to hear will nevermore
Walk side by side with mine through yonder door.
I listen, listen farther, farther back
The mocking echoes die along the track
She trod. Fain would I walk the golden street,
If she be there ; then haste, oh, haste, my feet !

Work swift, my hand !
The fingers that would clasp, and understand
Thy slightest motion, move no more for thee ;
Oh, swifter, swifter let thy working be !
For I would show the finished task to one
Whose arm embraced me when it was begun.
If she is resting in that happier land,
I soon would rest there ; then work swift, my hand !

Speak low, my voice !
The ear that at thy accents would rejoice,
And think thy tones were musical and sweet,
Can hear no more, till, at the end, we meet ;
Can hear no more, for, if she heard me now,
I think she 'd find some way to tell me how
My song is still the music of her choice.
But, near or far, speak low, sing low, my voice !

Beat quick, my heart !
Still faster, faster let the life depart !
My lonely soul would gladly try its wings,

And soar beyond these death-destroying things,
To heaven. I know not how, I know not where,
I only know the one I love is there,
And strange new life into my frame shall start
A life immortal ! Oh, beat quick, my heart !

THE PASSING OF TENNYSON.

SUNRISE and morning star
    Where evening shades had been,
And waving hands, and greetings from afar,
    When he went in.

Fresh leaves across the prow,
    And blossoms strangely fair,
And soft-breathed whispers, " Heaven is here and
    now,"
    Around him everywhere.

A breeze that brings from shore
    Fragrance immortal, sweet ;
Arms reaching shoreward, outward, more and more
    Till hands in clasping meet.

Sunrise and crimson east
    As morning bells begin,
And, through the dawning, one sweet smile at least,
    When he went in.

WHEN LEAVES ARE LYING LOW.

WHEN leaves are lying low
    Beneath October's tread,
Across the empty fields I go,
    Whose hopes are harvested,
Along a narrow, grass-grown way,
    Within a mossy gate,
Where dead leaves love so well to stay,
    Their falling I await.
"O! dear decaying leaves," I cry,
"What heavenly hopes beneath you lie!"

When leaves are lying low,
    And, crushed beneath my feet,
They turn to earth, I ought to know
    The lesson, once so sweet,
That autumn surely leads to spring,
    And leaflets rise from dust;
I see the vanished blossoming,
    And weep because I must.
"These leaves are dead, are dead," I say,
"And all my heart is dead to-day."

"New leaves shall spring, new leaves shall spring,"
    I hear it overhead;
It whispers in the boughs that fling
    Their dust above my dead.

"New leaves shall spring," the winds repeat;
  The brooklet sings it o'er:
"From death to life." O, hope so sweet!
  Stay with me evermore,
Till doubt beneath the leaves shall lie,
And new-born faith shall touch the sky.

THY WILL BE DONE.

THY will be done. O! can I say,
  My Father, this sweet prayer to-day?
When Thou dost lift the chastening rod,
Do I receive it as from God?
When dangers threaten, do I dare
Or long to follow anywhere
That Thou dost lead? When o'er my soul
The waves of sorrow fiercely roll,
Can I look up, through every one,
And say: O! Lord, Thy will be done?

Thy will be done. I want to say,
My Father, this sweet prayer to-day.
I want, but oh! the heart will ache,
And cannot help it. For Thy sake
I'll try; but I was made to miss
The hand in mine, the tender kiss;
When they are taken, how can I
Keep back the murmur? If I sigh,
And let the tears unbidden run,
Can I say then, Thy will be done?

Thy will be done. Lord ! help me say
This prayer, my Saviour's prayer, to-day.
Thou knowest best, Thou seest all,
If I cannot—I bend—I fall—
I throw my troubles at Thy feet ;
Lord, turn this bitter into sweet,
While I am tasting ; let me see
The good Thou hast prepared for me ;
Complete the work thou hast begun,
That I may say, Thy will be done.

Thy will be done. Yes, I can say
This prayer, some time, if not to-day.
For I am sure that Thou dost see
The path that leads from earth to Thee,
Though I see not. Reach down Thy hand
Among the shadows where I stand,
And lift me upward—if I must
Be blindfold, show me how to trust.
*   *   *   *   *   *
I catch one glimpse—oh ! blessed One,
Thy will be done, Thy will be done.

IN PART.

SKY ! soft sky !
    To thee I turn mine eye,
And read, the stars between,
One word of what thy glories mean.
And then, though much I need,
No more can read.

Wind, sweet wind!
Thy voice to-day is kind!
Thou whisperest in mine ear
Words that I just begin to hear;
Thou goest from east to west,
I lose the rest.

Earth, glad earth!
To thee I owe my birth;
In thy warm lap I sit,
Thy tender arms around me knit,
I question—Thou dost say
Now yea, now nay.

Soul, my soul!
Thou canst not know the whole;
The sky can know its star;
The breeze its perfume from afar;
The earth reveal to thee
One mystery!

But soul, my soul!
Thou soon shalt know the whole;
When earth and sea and sky
Have vanished, shall thine eye
Translate the book of fate;
Then wait, oh, wait!

MY PORTION.

O YEAR that bade this budding spring
    Set summer blossoms free !
Of all the bounties thou dost bring,
    What will my portion be ?

When grass peeps up from yonder sod,
    And snows to perfumes turn,
What thought will they reveal from God
    To make me heavenward yearn ?

When daisies dot the dales with white,
    Or buttercups, with gold,
What hope, to give my heart delight,
    Will blossoming unfold ?

When corn grows yellow in the fields,
    And grain is ripe to reap,
What blessings that the harvest yields,
    For me, will August keep ?

When all the rainbow of the wood,
    With gold or crimson gleams,
Shall I see visions grand and good,
    And tell the world my dreams ?

When withered leaves are lying low,
    And snow-flakes fill the air,
Shall I hear God in winds that blow,
    And know Him everywhere ?

O year that bade the budding spring
    Make summer petals grow !
Teach me to find in everything
    The good thou wouldst bestow.

Help me to touch the keys of truth,
    Till they shall answer me,
Then will thy smallest gifts, forsooth,
    An ample portion be.

HER BIRTHDAY.

YOUR birthday, darling ! Do you know
    I think about it ? That I go
From room to room, as if to see
If you have not come back to me ?

Upon the walls around, I place
In every room, the silent face
So like your own ; but, oh ! I miss
The warm, warm lips I used to kiss.

A costly gift, one year ago,
I planned to give you. Do you know
I thought of it ? Why did I wait
To give until it was too late ?

Your birthday, dear—oh ! could I see
How you are spending it ; could we,
For just one moment's space, look through
The veil which falls 'twixt me and you ;

If I could only push aside
This veil, and see where you abide,
Or help you, darling, celebrate
Your first birthday beyond the gate,

How gladly I the veil should lift,
And bear you some sweet birthday gift ;
How gladly I the tale should tell
Of all the year. Perhaps 't is well

I cannot do it, for my eye,
One glimpse would poorly satisfy ;
The curtain I should wish to tear,
And be with you forever there.

OCTOBER.

O crimson leaf ! Thy blush
   Makes glad the watching sky,
Till sunset clouds send back the flush
   In tints of roseate dye ;
And every withered plant or bush
   Looks up with envious eye.

O scarlet leaf ! Thy hue
   Flames over wood and hill ;
Thou art the old within the new,
   The bud remembered still ;
October fruits are made of dew
   That April petals spill.

Crimson or scarlet bough,
  Or leaf of burning gold,
Once living green, but shining now
  In colors manifold,
Your autumn glory tells me how
  True hearts grow grandly old.

A WINTER LULLABY.

THE valley has gone to sleep,
  The birds in their nests are still,
And the maple branches bend and weep
  Over the leafless hill,
Till the pitying sky looks down
  And whispers to the snow:
"Let us cover the hills so bare and brown
  Where the flowers used to grow."
And she croons a lullaby
  Through the hush of the storm :
    "Sleep, sleep, in your cradle deep
      I will keep you warm ;
    O, sleep, sleep, sleep !"

The valley is going to wake,
  The birds in their nests will sing,
And the maple buds begin to break
  Into the leaves of spring ;
For the dreaming vale will hear
  Another lullaby,

The zephyrs will whisper it into her ear
  Out of the heart of the sky,
Another cradle song
  Tuned to the harp of the stream:
    "Wake, wake
      For the robins' sake,
       And tell the sky your dream.
    O, wake, wake, wake!"

HOMEWARD.

YES, I am coming, coming to you:
  What is the light I have seen
Gilding my pathway, and guiding me through
  All the long desert between?
Darkness behind me, darkness around,
  Only the pathway is bright:
Lightly my footsteps are touching the ground—
  I shall be with you to-night.

Yes, I am coming, coming to you;
  What is the music I hear—
Filling the road I am clambering through,
  Growing each moment more clear?
Darkness behind me, darkness around,
  Yet I am filled with delight;
Through the dim distance is winding a sound,—
  I shall be with you to-night.

Yes, I am coming, coming to you ;
   What is the touch that I feel
Lifting me, drawing me ever anew,
   Even as the magnet the steel?
Onward, right onward, I airily bound ;
   Something is holding me tight ;
Helping me over the slippery ground,—
   I shall be with you to-night.

Is it the flash from the blue of your eye,
   Lighting my pathway along?
Does the long road, as I gayly draw nigh,
   Echo the trill of your song?
Ah ! how the outstretching arms of your love
   Draw me with infinite might !
Bliss is around and before and above,—
   Sweet ! I am with you to-night.

FREE.

AS a poor prisoner, in his narrow cell,
   I spend my years,
The reason I am here I cannot tell,
   But through my tears
I watch the captives, that for evermore
Go back and forth beside my prison door.

My prison walls are very thick and deep,
   Its windows high ;

Free.

Sometimes, on tiptoe, through the grates I peep
      With wondering eye,
And then upon the cold dark floor I fall,
And cannot tell what I have seen at all.

Sometimes I look above the iron bars,
      And dimly see
The shining of the sweet unfettered stars,
      And think may be
I too can learn what every freeman knows,
And then—the shutters of my prison close.

Sometimes there falls, through that unplastered
    chink,
      Upon the air,
The perfume of a rose or garden pink,
      And lingers there.
But, while I wonder whence the sweetness is,
Along the low, damp ground it vanishes.

Sometimes the distant note of summer bird
      I faintly hear;
With silent rapture all my soul is stirred,
      As it draws near,
But, farther, farther back the music flows;
I know not whence it comes, nor where it goes.

Sometimes a loving hand I seem to clasp,
      Compassionate,

Of one who's reaching for my tender grasp
    Outside the gate,
And then—I wake ; he is beyond the stars,
And I am pining still, behind the bars.

How long I must within my prison stay,
    I do not know ;
And when they tell me I shall leave, some day,
    I fear to go ;
For I have lived so long inside the cell,
I love its very darkness all too well.

So much I fear, that if to-night I heard
    The keeper say:
"You may go out," I should, with stammering word,
    Cry : "Let me stay ;
I ask for just one day's delay before
I shall be ready for the open door."

But hark ! I hear a step along the track—
    Why am I dumb ?
The key is turning now, the bolt flies back—
    He's come—he's come !
He opens wide the door—his face I see ;
" Poor captive," he is calling, "you are free !"

OH, FOR THE HILLS AGAIN!

"Oh, for the hills again! oh, for the hills again!"
  Came from the heart of the ocean;
"Give me the fountain side, give me the mountain side,
  Far from the billow's commotion;
There I was beautiful, there I was music full,
  Yes, if the raindrops but knew it.
Turn again, ebbing tides, back where my spring abides,—
  Ah! if they only could do it."

"Oh, for my youth again! oh, for my youth again!"
  Came from the heart burden breaking;
"Make me a boy once more, make me a child once more,
  Far from life's quaking and aching;
Then I was glad and free, then I was fancy free;
  Yes, if the children but knew it.
Turn again, dreary days! back where my childhood plays,—
  Ah! if they only could do it."

GOING ABROAD.

MY love and I from childhood planned
    To travel in a foreign land—
"When we are older," she would say,
"We 'll go abroad—there 'll be some way.

"We 'll go to Switzerland and France
And view the scenes of old romance,
And look at emperors and kings
And ruins, and all ancient things.

"We 'll visit England. We will see
The storied plains of Italy.
We 'll sail together down the Rhine
And close our trip with Palestine."

The years slipped by. We did not find
A time to go, but stayed behind
And labored while our neighbors went
Abroad—and so the years were spent.

And so we waited, toiled, and sung
Until we were no longer young,
But never travelled anywhere
Except to castles in the air.

   *   *   *   *   *   *

I woke from dreams one Sabbath day
To find my love had gone away.
A ship had come from parts unknown
And carried her abroad, alone.

I did not see the way she went,
To Orient, or Occident,
Toward Southern Cross, or Northern Star,
I do not know if near or far.

I only know that it must be
The same swift ship will come for me
And bear me sometime to the place
Where I can see her face to face.

I only know that I shall see
A fairer land than Italy;
And pleasures far more grand and pure,
Than any earthly foreign tour.

And so I wait the will of God
To stay at home or go abroad;
Contented if I only may
Go where my love has gone, some day.

SURE.

YES, we are sure
    That we shall see her, grown more sweet
        and pure,
And yet so like, that the first glance will show
The very darling that we used to know;
Sure we shall hasten to the outstretched hand,
And all the tangled past shall understand;
Shall tell the little story of the days
Since we have parted, taking different ways.

We're sure of this,
Even while we miss
The tender pressure of her morning kiss.

Yes, I am sure, but cannot yet be glad
That she is glad away from me ; the sad,
Sad tears (how can I help it) flow.
Because I love her, and I want her so.
Sometime I'll clasp my darling to my breast,
And find again the olden blessèd rest.
But oh ! the years are long ; I know not how
To wait.   I *want her now.*

THE AUTUMN MIRACLE.

O, wondrous miracle ! The autumn hills,
    That lately lifted sober tree-tops up,
Grow strangely glad.
             A loving Master fills
With sparkling radiance every leafy cup,
And all the woods and mountains seem to shine,
As if He turned their water into wine.

AN ORIENTAL WISH.

TRANSLATED FROM THE GERMAN.

WHEN first those dear eyes pierced the night,
    Thou didst weep,
While those around thee laughed, with new delight,
    A child to keep.

When last thou look'st upon the light,
    And death's long sleep
Approacheth, smiling, mayst thou say good-night,
    While others weep.

A WINTER FANCY.

THE Summer is fast asleep
    Under the winter snow ;
Her bed is warm, her bed is deep,
    Deeper than frosts can go.

She has slept for many a week ;
    O ! I wish she would awake !
I long for the blush of her rosy cheek,
    And the music she will make.

Sometimes, when the south wind blows,
    I fancy that I hear,
In the hush of the storm, an echo that goes
    Into my longing ear,

Like the trill of a robin's note,
    Or the murmur of growing things ;
On the frosty air it seems to float,
    Till it mounts on a snow-flake's wings.

" 'T is but the wind," they say,
    But my fancy I must keep ;
The Summer is pushing the snow away
    And talking in her sleep.

IF I KNEW WHERE.

WHERE, darling! Where
    Is heaven? Oh! tell me, now that you
      are there.
We asked the question but a year ago,
And did not dream that you so soon would know.
If I could know what hallowed part of space
Is my immortal darling's dwelling-place,
Life would be worth the living; I could bear
My burden better, till I meet you there,
If I knew where.

Is heaven a star?
The one that looks upon me now, so far
Above the shadows? Do these beams that shine
So clearly, come from your sweet home to mine?
I should be happier, then, if you could be
Within that radiance looking down on me,
And I could know it; through the midnight air,
Your joy, my darling, I could almost share,
If I knew where.

Is heaven here,
My glorified? and are you hovering near
To help me, guide me? Is it that we 're blind,
And deaf, and dumb, that we can never find
The heaven around us? Are you speaking now

A language to me, that I know not how
To hear or render? Close beside my chair,
Unseen by me, are angels ; here or there ?
Oh ! tell me where ?

It cannot be.
Nor earth nor star is heaven ; it seems to me,
Where " gates of gold " and " many mansions " rise,
In God's illimitable space it lies.
I will not ask you any more to tell
The sacred spot, for, oh ! I know too well
You dare not do it. Up the shining stair
Should I not hasten, or the curtain tear
If I knew where ?

And yet, and yet,
My darling, I do sometimes quite forget
That we are parted ; almost feel that I
Am still where you are ; sometimes even try
To hear your footstep. Oh, dear heart, dear heart,
My other self, my purer, better part,
How blest to meet you ! Father, hear my prayer !
Thou art beside me, keep me in Thy care,
Till I know where.

WAIT.

GUIDE of my upward path!
    Fain would I know
Sights of the mountain top
    Whither I go;
Paint thou on yonder sky
Pictures, beyond that lie.

Child! thou canst plainly see
All that is good for thee.

Guide of my upward path!
    Fain would I hear
Sounds from the other side,
    Tuneful and clear.
Is that the song they sing
Far upward echoing?

Wait, child! 'T will not be long
Ere thou shalt sing the song.

Guide of my upward path!
    Slowly I climb,
When shall I reach the top?
    Tell me the time?
How many summits rise
'Twixt me and yonder skies?

Child! thou the time shalt know;
Hilltops will lighter grow!

Guide of my upward path!
   Close to the skies
Will a lost hand reach down
   Helping me rise?
Will lips that love me wait
Just by the open gate?

Climb, child! and thou shalt see
All that is kept for thee.

LOWLAND MUSIC.

HIGHER! Still higher!
   My hungry heart cries out. My strong
     desire
Spurs me to mount the hilltops; though my feet
Have never scaled one slope. It would be sweet
To climb unto the stars; to see, to know
All I have longed for; would be good to go
Far up those heights, and place my humble name
Above the rest upon the crags of fame.
Come, sacred muse, my thought, my lips inspire!
I would mount higher.

Higher! Still higher!
Your heart cries out.
     Child! Why should you inquire
The way to mount?
      Ah, dullard! have you seen
All that is lying 'neath the valley's green?
Ere you shall turn toward yonder cliff-pierced sky,
Survey the lowly valley where you lie;
Look in these nooks; see how the wild-flowers
 bloom;
Keep step to lowland music; drink perfume.
Then may you mount by your attuned lyre
Higher! Still higher!

OUTSIDE.

O, distant, near, mysterious land,
 Where all my household stay!
Upon thy vestibule I stand
 At dying of the day,
And watch the shadows come and go
 Across the close-shut bars,
And listen for a voice I know,
 Beneath the voiceless stars.

The curtain lifts, and, from above,
 Familiar fire-lights fall
Upon my face; the ones I love
 Are just behind it all.

I rush to meet! The light goes out,
  If there were any there.
I listen—linger—all about
  Is silence everywhere.

O, glorious home! O, mystery!
  O, home that shall be mine!
What is that immortality
  Beyond thy doors divine?
In vain I lift my hand to knock,
  Or strain mine eyes to see;
I wait unanswered at the lock,
  Till Death shall turn the key.

DIVIDED.

SPIRIT, adieu! the Body said,
  As Death stood waiting by the bed;
The pains of parting rack me so,
I wish, I long for thee to go;
Oh, hasten, Spirit! it is best
For thee to go, for me to rest.

Where dost thou go, my Spirit, say?
Is it a long and weary way?
Or is it near, so near, that I
May feel thy presence where I lie
Beneath the summer sod asleep?
How strange a silence thou dost keep!

We have been long together, sweet,
In loving fellowship ; 't is meet
That we should whisper, ere we part,
Some tender words ; this faithful heart
Has beat for thee, so fast, so slow,
So long—but now go, Spirit, go !

Yes, go ! but shouldst thou ever yearn
For old companionship, or turn
From heaven to earth, then come and bend
Awhile above thy life-long friend,
Till, from some leaf, or bud, or flower,
My answering dust shall feel thy power.

But stay ! It is so hard to part !
Another beating of the heart !
Just one fond whisper, and I must
Go back to pulseless, voiceless dust !
Enough ! Take thou thine upward quest !
We meet again, but now, I *rest*.

A BROKEN DREAM.

I DREAMED, it was a dream. I saw her face
   Still smiling on me from the same old place
She used to wait me.
              "Is it you, my dear ? "
I asked. She answered, " Darling, I am here."

I ran into her arms, I clasped her tight,
I whirled her round and round in wild delight.
She talked. I listened, listened, laughed and wept,
The while my arms around her neck I kept.
" I dreamed that you were dead ; oh ! can it be
That you are really here so close to me ?"
" Forgive my olden foolish words," I plead ;
" I have forgotten every word," she said.
" Poor child ! Poor child ! and so you dreamed I
    died.
Look ! I am here. Are you not satisfied ?"
And, as she closer to my heart-beats crept
Until I heard her own, I dreamed I slept.—
I woke at morn ; O God ! she was not there,
My lips were kissing into empty air.
A broken dream—But oh ! my glad lips thrill,
Though days have passed, with her lips' pressure
    still.
Easter, 1889.

MARY LYON.

SHE did not ask
    To be released from any toilsome task,
Asked not for wealth or fame or human love ;
The only prayer her parted lips above
Was this :
      "O Father, show me how to be
Faithful in heart and life, each day, to Thee."

She did not fear
The world's remark; she heeded not its sneer;
Feared not to bear her burden up the height,
If she were sure each upward step was right;
Her only fear, she "might not fully know
Her duty and perform it daily." So
Her cup of days,
Though spilled at noontime, brimmed with good
    men's praise;
Her thought took root, and bud and blossom bore,
And sweet rich fruit of kind unknown before.
Success and love and God's sweet comfort came
To her in life.
        Undying is her fame.

THOUGHT'S TRYST.

WE sat together, at the twilight hour,
    Beneath the chestnut tree,
We walked together in the morning cool,
    We three.

    We studied morals from the same dry book,
        And when our task was done,
    We went together to our trysting-place,
        Room one.

    Mingling our tears of parting, at the end,
        We went our separate ways,
    And vowed we 'd never for an hour forget
        Those days.

Thought's Tryst.

One in the land of roses found a home;
  One, under northern pines;
The other marked upon the dark-land shore
      Her lines.

Never a word or message do we send
  O'er land or sea,
We are too busy; life has too much work
      For memory.

Never a word or letter do we send;
  Ah! we forget,
In all the whirl and weariness of life,
      And yet—

Sometimes, at twilight hour, our labor over,
  Our work we fold,
And wonder what has come to those we cherished
      Of old.

A tender thought from fragrant pine-tree branches
  Flies o'er the snow;
Far, far across the sea, to dark-land fountains
      It goes.

A tender thought floats down the northern streamlet
  To southern streams,
And asks for just one hour of dreaming
      Old dreams.

Oh! that our distant thoughts, to-night, might
    gather,
From land or sea,
And we might *think* we *sat beneath the chestnut*—
    We three.

AT WORK.

TO S. R. M.

THE year is rising from its winter rest,
    The spring is nigh,
The bird is dreaming of its summer nest,
    While you and I

Must leave the shelter of our cottage door,
    Its warmth and cheer,
And go to work as we have done before
    For many a year.

Beyond the brook, a shadow seems to fall.
    We will not weep,
But upward look, and thank the Lord for all
    We still may keep.

The village roofs above the snow-drifts peep
    To see the sun ;
Be patient, violets, for your winter's sleep
    Is almost done.

The hanging bough its old sweet robin sees,
  That went away
And left her cradle empty in the trees
  One autumn day.

The children wait within their last year's seats,
  While you and I
Are like the birds : each year the same repeats
  In school and sky.

Come here, my girls ! my boys ! swing back the door,
  And ring the bell ;
Your coming feet make music on the floor,
  And all is well.

AT REST.

TO S. R. M.

THE rolling year draws near its golden noon
    And all the air
Is fragrant with the rosy breath of June,
    While here and there
The robins twitter in their blue-egged nests,
    The earth is green,
Soft silver clouds glide down the mountain crests,
    The hills between
Are brimmed with music, sunshine, summer flowers,
    And you and I

Will drink the sweetness of the passing hours,
    And say " Good-bye."
Good-bye, dear happy girls, and merry boys ;
    Lock up the door
Of our old schoolhouse, empty of its noise ;
    As oft before
The elm-trees call me to their grateful rest ;
    Begone, dull care.
The cottage door is open ; it is blest
    To enter there.
Come, sister, come, put by the book and slate,
    The ink and pen,
The kittens at the homely doorstep wait,
    'T is June again !

LOST—MY BOY.

LOST ! I have lost him.
    When did he go ?
Lightly I clasped him,
    How could I know
Out of my dwelling
    He would depart—
Even as I held him
    Close to my heart !

Lost ! I have lost him.
    Somewhere between
Schoolhouse and college
    Last he was seen,

Lost—My Boy.

Lips full of whistling,
   Curl-tangled hair ;
Lost ! I have lost him.
   Would I knew where.

Lost ! I have lost him.
   Chester, my boy !
Picture-book, story-book,
   Marble and toy,
Stored in the attic,
   Useless they lie.
Why should I care so much ?
   Mothers, tell why.

Yes, he has gone from me ;
   Left me no sign,
Save that another
   Calls himself mine.
Handsome and strong of limb,
   Stately is he ;
Knows things that I do not ;
   Who can it be ?

Face like the father's face ;
   Eyes black as mine,
Step full of manly grace,
   Voice masculine.
Yes, but the gold of life
   Has one alloy ;
Why does the mother-heart
   Long for her boy ?

> Long for the mischievous
>   Queer little chap,
> Ignorant, questioning,
>   Held in my lap.
> Freshman, so tall and wise,
>   Answer me this:
> Where is the little boy
>   I used to kiss?

TRANSPLANTED.

A THOUGHT FROM PHILLIPS BROOKS.

LIKE Southern plants removed to Northern climes,
    That strive to grow,
And dimly dream of blossoms, oftentimes,
    But do not know

The way to make them: now, a tiny bud,
    A blighted bloom,
Betrays the inner longing, tropic blood,
    And lost perfume.

So we, poor earthly exiles from our own,
    In weakness try
To put forth actions that our dreams have known,
    And know not why

The power is lacking—do not even know
    What we have done,
Though vaguely conscious life doth never show
    The perfect one.

"Oh! for our native soil, so warm and sweet!"
    We sometimes say,
But strive our lost ideals to complete
    As best we may.

And shall we reach them?
              Yes; from hour to hour,
    Even as we try,
So surely to the heaven-born perfect flower
    We shall draw nigh.

And, by-and-by, O, yes! I do believe
    There is a day,
Life's rose transplanted, shall the power receive
    To bloom alway.

LOVING ECHOES.

PRAISE, and the world will heed you,
    Blame, and it heeds you not,
For a word of praise in the memory stays,
    Never to be forgot;

Or, if chiding be remembered,
   It is only for its sting,
But loving words, like songs of birds,
   Are forever echoing.

Look for the fragrant roses,
   Not for the thorns and weeds,
For the crimson sky, when night is nigh,
   And the golden sun recedes.
Glistens the Starry Dipper,
   Sparkles the Milky-Way,
Through midnight trees, the clear eye sees
   Glimpses of dawning day.

Kisses but not upbraidings,
   The smile but not the frown,
For the love must be deep that afloat will keep,
   If harshness press it down ;
Like the falling dews of summer,
   Or the welcome autumn rain,
Kind words may flow from the lips, and go
   To the skies of the heart again.

Praise, and your friend will hear you,
   Blame, and he heeds you not,
For a word of praise in the memory stays,
   Never to be forgot ;
But if chiding be remembered,
   It is only for its sting,
And loving words, like songs of birds,
   Are forever echoing.

A STAR CAN BE AS PERFECT AS A SUN.

BECAUSE you cannot be
  An overhanging bow,
Whose promise all the world can see,
  Why are you grieving so?
A dew-drop holds the seven colors too;
Can you not be a perfect drop of dew?

Because you cannot be
  Resplendent Sirius,
Whose shining all the world can see,
  Why are you grieving thus?
One tiny ray will reach out very far;
Can you not be a perfect *little* star?

The smallest, faintest star
  That dots the Milky-Way,
And sends one glimmer where you are,
  Gives forth a faultless ray;
Learn then this lesson, oh, discouraged one!
A star can be as perfect as a sun.

THE HAPPY CHOICE.*

HAPPINESS! happiness!
   How shall I find?
Perfect, unchangeable,
   Free as the wind?
Fame? it abideth not,
   Power? it will sting,
Gold? as it glittereth
   Joy taketh wing.
Take what is offered thee child, from above—
                      Choose Love.

If in the desert soil
   Love's rootlet grows,
Soon is the blossoming
   Sweet as the rose;
Love that can change a sigh
   Into a song—
Generous, compassionate,
   Suffering long.
Lift up thy hand to this gift from above—
                      Choose Love.

By and by, singing birds
   Finding a nest

---

* Suggested by an article in a late magazine, written by Mrs. K. D. Wiggin.

The Happy Choice.

Close to thy happy heart,
    Thou shalt find rest—
Rest glad and comforting,
    Though it should be,
Wings that are tipped with gold
    Fly *over* thee.
Lift up thine eyes to this gift from above—
                    Choose Love.

Shall I grow weary then
    After a while?
Tired of the melody,
    Tired of the smile?
Weary, but not of love—
    Ask me not why
Life has its thunder-clouds,
    Even as the sky.
Soon thou shalt see the sun shining above—
                    Choose Love.

Life is not all complete;
    Earth is not heaven;
Life is not all unrest,
    If love be given.
Though the bright sun be hid,
    Shadowed in doubt,
Live by love's candle light,
    Blow it not out.
Wait, and the morning will break from above—
                    Choose Love.

Flowers shall spring up for thee,
    Perfumed with peace,
Even when the morning sun
    Seemeth to cease ;
Love shall illuminate
    Darkening years,
Love shall still keep for thee
    Kisses and tears.
Hold up thy hand, my child ! Reach it above—
                    Choose Love.

Love, as of friend for friend,
    Faithful and true ;
Love, like a mother's heart
    Beating for you.
Love, like a brother's love,
    Tender and strong ;
Love, like a lover's love,
    Thinking no wrong.
Love the immortal, sent down from above—
                    Choose Love.

SAYS I AND SAYS HE.

SAYS I to the Deacon, says I :
    The world is what you make it :
Give your neighbor a cuff and he 'll try
    To cuff you back, I take it.
But give him a helpin' hand,
    In plantin' time or in hoein',

An keep your critters off' on his land,
   He never will be throwin'
Stones acrost—so it 'pears to me.
" That's so, that's so," says the Deacon, says he.

Says I to the Deacon, says I :
   The Bible is all of it true, sir,
As good to read as to practise by,
   For people like me an' you, sir,
But I tell ye, I'd like to know
   Why all o' the parson's preachin',
An' all his prayin', an' so an' so,
   Is n't no further reachin'
Into the pockets o' you an' me,
" Ahem, ahem," says the Deacon, says he.

Says I to the Deacon, says I :
   This talkin' about probation,
An' sendin' the Andover folks so high,
   Is a terrible aggravation
To peaceable people, tryin' to do
   As we'd like to have done to us ;
It seems to me, don't it seem to you,
   They are makin' a terrible fuss,
Lawin' an' prayin' don't agree.
" That's so, that's so," says the Deacon, says he.

Says I to the Deacon, says I :
   You are havin' a heap o' trouble,

An' I s'pose you think, by the way you sigh,
    Your share is more than double;
But I tell you what I think;
    If you was neighbor Jack, sir,
You 'd swap with yourself as quick as a wink,
    An' be glad o' your own big pack, sir;
Your troubles might be bigger 'n they be.
" Taint so, taint so," says the Deacon, says he.

Says I to the Deacon, says I:
    I am tryin' a brand new plan—
To take things just as they come, an' try
    To be as happy as I can;
An' the notion 's workin' well,
    For the neighbors are 'mazin' kind;
An' I think if you 'd try it yourself a spell
    You 'd be of a cheerfuller mind;
'T would be better for you, as it is for me.
" Dunno, dunno," says the Deacon says he.

Says the Deacon to me, says he;
    " I 'm a thorough-bred Orthodox,
But it don't appear to be hinderin' me
    From gettin' some master hard knocks;
An' as to the great dispute,
    I never was half so good
At a splittin' hairs like Parson Nute
    As at splittin' kindlin' wood;
An' I think 't would be better for you an' me
To be lookin' to home," says the Deacon, says he.

A WEDDING SONG.

K. M. AND H. A.

WHAT gilds the mountain tops,
    Last year so gray?
What is the murmuring brook
    Singing to-day?
Ah! 'T is your thoughts, my love,
    Gild the high peaks;
" Love is the best of all,"
    Thus the brook speaks.
Sing of a love so sweet murmuring springs,
Whitening the mountain tops with Cupid's wings.

What paints the lily cup,
    Last year so pale?
What new sweet breath creeps up
    On the soft gale?
Ah! 'T is your thought, my love,
    New brightness sees;
" Love is the best of all,"
    Floats on the breeze.
Lily and fragrant rose say unto you:
" Old things have passed away, all things are new."

What lights the sky of eve,
    Last year so dark?

What calms the billow's heave
    Under my bark?
Ah! 'T is your thoughts my love
    Crimson the sky;
Love's breezes float your boat
    Merrily by.
Enter the heaven of bliss, haven of rest;
"Love is the best of all, love is the best."

MOTHER'S GIRL.

SHE sits securely by my side,
    My bonny little lass!
The world is cold, the world is wide,
    I let the cold world pass;
With Mary smiling up at me,
I care not what the world may be.

She looks into my faded face,
    My bonny little lass!
But does not see the wrinkled place
    Where time's rough footsteps pass;
She measures me by love's own rule,
And thinks, "Mamma is beautiful."

She asks me many curious things,
    My bonny little lass!
"Be angels shaking out their wings?"
    She says, when snow-showers pass.

I kiss her happy face and say :
" Angels have surely passed this way."

She looks at me with curious eyes,
   My bonny little lass !
Queer little questions quaintly stir
   The rippling words that pass.
" Is God a Quaker ? 'Cause, you know,
He Thees and Thous the verses so."

She holds her head against my breast,
   My bonny little lass !
Her eyelids droop, her tired lips rest,
   Her thoughts to dreamland pass ;
While bending down to kiss that curl,
I hear her whisper, " Mother's girl."

WHEN MERRY SLEIGH BELLS RING.

WHEN merry sleigh bells ring
   So silvery, soft and sweet,
When all the fields are answering
   Till blending echoes meet,
Along the road I climb, I climb,
And as I climb I sing—
     To their glad chime ;
   Oh ! happy time,
When merry sleigh bells ring.

I see far down the vale,
   The river wrapped in snow ;
But sometimes peeping to inhale
   The breath of winds that blow,
And now the river winds and winds,
And now seems listening,
      But half resigned
      To be confined,
When merry sleigh bells ring.

A bit of shining crust
   Holds down the feathery flakes
Beside me ; far beneath the dust,
   No sleeping bud awakes ;
But as the children shout and shout,
I mind me of the spring,
      For all about,
      Fresh joys leap out,
When merry sleigh bells ring.

Till back I come and sit,
   And hear the tinkling sound ;
I watch the forms that float and flit
   Above the icy ground.
And "Oh ! the world is bright, is bright ! "
My fingers seem to sing ;
      My pen moves light
      From left to right,
When merry sleigh bells ring.

WINTER VIOLETS.

SOMETIMES for an hour in December,
   We seem to catch glimpses of May,
And we smile as we fondly remember
   The nooks where the violets stay ;
Just over the bank by the river,
   Safe under the sheltering snows,
They are waiting, as onward forever
   The invisible rivulet flows.

Sometimes in life's chilly December
   We seem to catch glimpses of spring,
And the snows only make us remember
   That they cover the blossoming,
For as under the drifts of the meadow
   Wild flowers may be pushing through,
So we smile as we see the shadow
   Of the old underneath the new.

Under the leaf is the blossom,
   Beneath the tear is the smile ;
And the earth conceals in its bosom
   The seed but a little while ;
Under the foot of the snow-drift,
   Is a budding anemone ;
And under the ice of death, the rift
   Of immortality.

LIVING STILL.

DOES he live yet? The home he fondly planned
    Long years ago, is resting on the land
Where he beheld it. Yonder spreading tree
Is the same one he planted, and the three
Stand in a line, just as the twigs were set,
When, by his loving hand, their roots were wet.
The bush he planted lives, and thrives, and grows,
And bears each passing year his favorite rose.
And shall the thing he planned so long endure,
And he live not? Ah, no; dear heart! Be sure,
Although that throbbing heart has long been still,
The soul above it is the same, and will
Sometime assert its own. My eyes are wet
With tears, but not for him,—He's living yet.

THAT BLESSED SPRING.

WHEN the winter of lifetime has melted away,
    And the song of the robin awakes,
When the hilltops are bright with the blossoms of
    May,
    And the spring of eternity breaks,
How the hearts that are longing, with gladness shall
    glow,
    As the love-scented winds out of Paradise blow!

Then hasten, O life ! from the bud to the bloom,
  From the bloom to the golden-hued leaf.
Let the roses drop downward, the harvest have room,
  And the joy-bells of Christmas be brief.
Fall fast, winter snowflakes ! for oh ! I would see
The Easter Immortal that's waiting for me.

OH, SUMMER SKY !

OH, Summer Sky ! The Arab told
    His fortune from thy stars of gold ;
The Hebrew shepherd smiled to view
This very shade of crystal blue,
When watching in Judean fold ;
I look to thee with heart less bold,
And long to learn some lesson new
From star or cloud of violet hue,
    Oh, Summer Sky !

But lo ! I see the heavens enrolled
In constellations, as of old ;
The self-same stars Hipparchus knew,
Sparkle on this fresh drop of dew,
This rosebud does to thee uphold,
    Oh, Summer Sky !

LIFE.

OH, Life! How short thou art!
    Short, though so sweet!
Short is the backward path
    Trod by my feet;
Short is the path ahead,
    Swiftly I go;
Whither my steps have led
    Soon I shall know;
Soon shall we know, dear heart!
Life! oh, how short thou art!

Oh, Life! how short thou art!
    Let me look back!
Tear drops! ye need not start!
    What do I lack?
Short is the road I've tried,
    Hilltops I see,
Over the other side
    Soon I shall be;
Soon shall be there, dear heart!
Life! oh, how short thou art!

A RONDEAU. THE CHILD AND THE RIVULET.

RIVULET ! Crystally clear !
    Under the wing of the shade !
What are you looking for here,
Running on, year after year,
  Out of the mountain cascade ?
Looking for springs bubbling near ?
    Watching how violets are made ?
    Listening for showers in the glade ?
                 Rivulet ?

Little maid ! sweet and sincere !
  Shower-scented violets may fade,
If you will drop me one tear,
The voice I am listening for here,
  Is yours. Down the valley conveyed,
'T will echo forever, my dear !
                  Rivulet.

SONNETS.

SONNETS.

TRUST.

A LITTLE girl came home from school one day,
    Holding within her hands a pretty weed,
And saying : " Mamma, once it was a seed,
And then it burst itself, and right away,
It peeped above the ground ; God let it stay
Where it could see the sky."
                      " When did you read
That story, pet," I asked. "I did n't need
To read "
        she said ;
                "I heard my teacher say
'T was so."
        Dear child ! if we the One who knows
Believed, like you ! when seeds forgotten lie,
" Out of the dark divinest beauty grows,"
Could say :
        " And, blinded, seeks the sunlit sky "—
Ah ! could we trust, not that the whole we know,
But simply that the Master told us so.

POSSESSION.

MY neighbor's meadow just across the way
   Is broader than my humble hillside field,
More golden grain or barley it can yield,
But does it wear a brighter green to-day?

At morn Aurora's life-reviving ray
   Tips all my rugged lands with fiery gold,
Before it shines upon my neighbor's hay,
Or warms the lambs within his ample fold.

And though his lofty elm and willow trees
   Are grand to him and to the passer-by,
Far more it does my simple nature please,
   To feast upon these apple-trees mine eye.
My neighbor thinks his intervale is fine;
I like my orchard better—It is mine.

SING AND LOOK UP.

AN early bird flew back, one April day,
   To cold New England fields, remembered well
When dressed in summer green.   Clear as a bell,
She sang: "To-weet, to-weet, 't is almost May."
And then she ceased. White drifts piled up the way

Where'er the singer looked ; she rose and fell,
Lightly she touched the empty ice-bound cell,
Where last year's birdlings learned their lay
From her own lullaby.
                        Beak toward the sun,
Again she gladly trilled ;
                    " To-weet, to-weet,
If I but wait the winter will be done ;
To-weet, to-weet, how happy I shall be ! "
Ah ! snow-bound heart, the long days have begun,
" Sing and look up, " the bird is telling thee.

RECOGNITION.

A SONNET FOR M. G.

A LONELY exile from your native cot
    In Switzerland, you look in every face
To find a friend. Perchance with joy you trace
In some new countenance the likeness sought
And cry, " It is a Swiss ! " Then scenes forgot
Return, and you are back a little space,
In glacier-watered Berne. You pass the place
Where home-folks live, and walk the very spot
Where childhood ran. Even thus, my friend, do we
Earth-exiled meet. Surprised, awhile we stand
Till I can trace in you (Do you in me ?)
The Master's face, and cry as hand clasps hand,
" A countryman ! " The *family look* we see,
And talk together of the Father-land.

THE OLD PETITION.

WE pray that sorrow may not touch our friends :
God hears, but sends the pain.
               We pray for cure,
Or that the tried soul bravely may endure,
And, even while we pray, the suffering ends
In death ; our quivering lip still upwards sends
The old petition :   Through the dim obscure
We raise our cries for those who are more pure
And glad than we can think, for parting rends
Our souls so deeply, we do quite forget,
Upon our knees, that all our darling's need
Of help is past.
           Oh ! while our eyes are wet
With fresh-fallen grief, and while torn heart-strings
    bleed,
I think the Heavenly Father will not care
If, for our lost, we breath the *same old prayer.*

SUCCESS.

A. M.

BACK to his childhood home he came,
    Having been absent one and forty years.
He left with empty purse and dropping tears,
And carried no ancestral honored name.

He had come back :
                  The village was the same,
The parsonage, the valleys, and the hills,
The mountain peaks, the murmur of the rills,
The western sunset with its radiant flame ;
But on his manly face was printed now
A story that his childhood never told.
" No need have I to show the people how
My dross of life was turned to shining gold ;
Faith, hope, and love, a purpose firm and free,
Have honored my nativity in me."

OPPORTUNITY.

"IT might have been," he sadly said to me,
    And threw himself upon the grassy ground,
And picked up withered leaves that floated round.
" It might have been, alas, it cannot be !
Put back the fallen twigs upon that tree,
For evening sunset change the morning glow,
Bring back your rosy cheek,—tell me to go
And push the coming tide into the sea,
But that lost chance I never can regain."
I pointed to the swinging boughs above,
And said : " New leaves are there, and still remain
Fresh opportunities for fame and love ;
The spring-times come and go eternally.
Arise—It might have been and it may be."

THE OLD CLOCK.

UNCHANGING record of the changing days!
    Still backward, forward, ticks thy pendulum,
That, for a century has swayed.
               Springs come
And go—swift summers pass, and autumn lays
Her fruit upon the lap of earth, nor stays
To join the Christmas feast.
               The busy hum
Of home thou heedest not, nor lips grown dumb
With grief, while round thy moon-faced dial's ways
The seconds march: Those leaden weights were wound
By hands that fought the king.
               How proud thy swing!
As if thy thoughts were, like thy years, profound,
And all the buried past could backward bring.
Four generations ticked into the ground,
Is it not time to stop thy winding string?

THE AWAKING.

AS a sweet baby from his morning dream
    Awakes, sometimes, and lies without a sound,
And all his rose-bud fingers twirl around
The while his violet eyes, half open, seem

Their petals to unfold, and pink cheeks beam
As if glad thoughts the little brain had found;
But when the mother's step upon the ground
He hears, his red lips speak the word supreme
In mothers' hearts—" Agoo!"
       So, we shall rise,
Perchance, when we awake from life's brief sleep,
Not all at once, but lie in rapt surprise,
And eye and lip all motionless shall keep,
Until we speak, as new-born powers expand,
Some glad strange word that God shall understand.

A NEW-YEAR'S SONNET.

O GLAD New Years! How rapidly ye rush
  To yonder ocean! Like a fountain's play
Ye seemed of yore; now, like a cataract's sway,
From month to month the onward minutes push.
My June day rose has hardly learned to blush
Before its petals wither; harvest day
And Christmas evening and the jingling sleigh
Of cold December mingle with the crush
Of April thunder.
    If at morn I lie
To hear again the voice of summer's song,
Behold the scarlet leaves go fluttering by!
Years, ye are mingling in a mighty throng!
Oh, stop a little while, and let me try
To pick the blossoms as I move along!

OUT-DOOR MUSIC.

THE windows of my soul fly open wide
    Sometimes, and thoughts rush forth, like
      birds set free
From cage, that almost seem to carry me
To Heaven.
         Upon the clouds awhile I ride,
My vision widened, strengthened, purified,
And then the sashes drop; I cannot see;
Each dingy pane reveals obscurity,
And serves one purpose only to divide
My soul from light.
           Oh, that I understood
The way to keep the glass at night so clear
The stars would always find me !
              If I could
Learn how to lift the windows till I hear
The out-door music, surely living would
Be happier, better.—
         Can you tell me, dear ?

THROUGH TRUST.

BENEATH Mt. Holyoke elms, sometimes, I
    stand,
And, glancing at the glorious evening sky,
One distant, starless, vacant spot descry,
That drops down darkness on the shining land ;

But if I cross the common, place the grand
Strong telescope before my lifted eye,
And strive that mystic void to magnify,
Behold! ere half the widening space is scanned,
A sparkling host appears.
      And thus I think
We look, beloved, toward the Eternal Blue,
Some gloomy grief this side; toward earth we shrink,
And say,
  "How dark!"
      We'll mount; we'll look anew
Through trust, and our expanded vision will
Life's far-off sky with twinkling glory fill.

FROM PAGE TO PAGE.

LIFE is a book in two grand volumes writ;
 The first read here, the second yonder; great
The themes in each, and all inadequate
Our finite minds to grasp the infinite,
Or read its chapters now.
     If, bit by bit,
We read, examine, reason, meditate
On every word of this, we can translate
The other by and by. Why then omit
That sentence hard, or glance above, below,
From page to page, or long to look ahead,
Or try to turn the leaves that you may know
The sequel of the second part, instead
Of giving careful study, as you go,
To every line until the volume's read?

LIFTED.

LIFE is a cradle, where the soul must lie
    And gather strength for its immortal years.
We sleep—we wake—shed unavailing tears
For fancied troubles, while we vainly try
To reach outside, or strain our feeble eye
Across the distant darkness.
                      All our fears
God knows ; His ear turns earthward when He
    hears
Our cries ; and, oh ! the mother's lullaby
Is not so sweet as Heaven's.
                      Then murmur not,
Sad soul, that in the cradle long hast lain;
A step draws near—God's child is not forgot ;
Ask not among the pillows to remain !
Soon, soon, shalt thou, oh, life-renewing thought !
Be lifted to the enfolding arms again.

TO J. E. S.

O friend ! to whom I showed, but yesterday,
    My inmost heart ! your listening ear I miss ;
I bend to hear your voice ; I think your kiss
Is on my lip.
           My pen I put away.

Sometimes, and softly to myself I say,
"To-morrow I will tell her this, and this,"
Forgetting you have entered into bliss,
And need me not; forgetting that I may
Not read my poem, that is almost done,
And hear your gentle comment, "It is good,"
Or
    "Make that better."
                      Ah! no other one
Would care to listen, nor have understood
The far beginning of the tales I 've spun;
None keep for me the heart of motherhood.

UNCERTAINTY.

IF I could only know, this very day,
  What the dim future holds within its store,
And if my portion should be less or more;
If I could know, with perfect certainty,
What work I ought to choose, what rocky way
Or flowery path my wandering feet should tread,
What suns or storms should fall upon my head
Before December took the place of May,
I should be satisfied to walk the road
Which had been marked by heavenly hand for me,
To take with willing heart my sweet abode
In country home, or cottage by the sea;
But, oh! I often see not what to do,
And murmur, "Father! if I only knew!"

SEAWARD.

FROM west to east, perchance, we gaily ride
    Some summer morning.
                      As we onward go,
And watch the fields, and towns, and cities, lo!
They all seem backward moving.
                      At our side
The traveller does not stir, but westward glide
Men, women, children, prairies, brooks that glow
In early sunlight—all sweet things that grow,
While we sit still.
               And thus we seem to bide
On life's brief journey ; till we think, may be,
Our little world has backward bent.
                      We smile,
Or weep, when forms familiar fade or flee,
And say : "How things do change !" "How earth
    grows vile !"
"How dark !" when, to the twilight of the sea,
'T is we alone are moving all the while.

AURORA.

THE morn walks gaily down the eastern hills,
    And lifts the rosy curtain of the sky ;
Upon the land she turns her flashing eye,
And all her fragrant breath the valley fills ;
She sprinkles sunshine on the sparkling rills,

And looks for corners where the daisies lie ;
Or lingers where the orioles flit by,
And drops fresh songs into their open bills ;
She wakes the maiden from her summer dream,
And calls the singing laborer from his bed ;
And lends the buttercups new tints, that seem
To take their colors from her golden head ;
And tunes the voices of the wood and stream,
And follows where the starry night has fled.

UNSATISFIED.

BLIND, blind from very birth was I,
    But always happy ; heaven and earth were kind,
Gladness kept watch above me ; for I did not try
    Nor care to see, not knowing I was blind.

I gained my sight, I saw a little way
    About my path ; the summer fields were green,
And stars were radiant. Why was I not gay
    As I had been before my eyes had seen
The rainbow or the rose ? I am not blind,
    Not wholly blind ; and yet I often weep
Because I see no farther. All my mind
    Is racked with wonder. If I try to sleep,
Strange light peeps through my half-shut lids, and I
Arise at morn—unsatisfied, unblest.
    " Oh, for the happy days ! " I sometimes cry,
" The days of blindness, ignorance, and rest ! "

PERSONAL POEMS.

FOR MY FRIENDS.

PERSONAL POEMS.

GRANDMOTHER'S FLOWER.*

FOR MRS. JULIA W. BUTLER.

UNDER the fragrant alcove
   Where her cherished flowers bloom,
Watching the tender smilax shoot,
   Or the ivy round the room,
She sings: "Oh, my beautiful flowers,
   My lily and columbine,
Jasmine and rose and japonica,
   I love you, and you are mine!"

"Oh, my fuchsia, rich and bright,
   And my rare geranium,
My pansy that turns to find the light,
   My white chrysanthemum!
I have watched your threading roots,
   I have bent your graceful stems,
I have trimmed your branches, trained your vines;
   You are more to me than gems."

* Mary Butler Thwing.

"Bright-eyed daisy buds
  Out in the garden grow,
The woods are full of sweet wild-flowers,
  That is their place to grow;
I would not ask for these,
  Let them be bright and strong,
Beneath the shelter of the trees,
  In nooks where they belong."

"The flowers I love to tend
  Are those that need my care.
The drooping slip I long to help,
  Or make the faded fair.
Oh, my sweet and beautiful flowers,
  My lily and columbine,
My pink and rose and japonica,
  I love you, and you are mine!"

Under the fragrant alcove,
  Where her cherished flowers blow,
Watching she tends another plant,
  And smiles to see it grow.
And she sings:
            "Oh, my precious blossom!
  My all sweet flowers in one!
Your lips to me are roses red,
  Your eyes fringed gentian,
Your breath is mignonette,
  Your neck the lily bell,
Your arms my ivy clinging yet,
  And you, my immortelle."

"Beneath these buds and flowers,
   I gave, one year ago,
My dearest plant to one who said,
   'My garden needs it so.'
Orange blossoms bright,
   Smiles, and a marriage bell,
Prayers, and tears, and vows of right,
   And now, an immortelle."

Singing still lower, softer,
   "May the Lord our darling keep,"
Grandma's voice is silent now,
   Baby has gone to sleep;
One more look at the flowers,
   When her pleasant task is done,
Then a whisper across the cradle low,
   "This is the fairest one."

FOURTEEN HAPPY YEARS.*

Fourteen happy years
   We've wound along the path, through smiles and tears,
While you have held me, husband, by the hand
And drawn me gently toward the mountain land;
If I was weary, on your faithful breast
I always found a refuge and a rest.

   * Written for Mrs. Helen C. Beedy on the death of her husband.

The journey, darling, has been very sweet;
The joy you gave, so constant, so complete,
That all the time before it, disappears
Beneath the radiance of these happy years.

Fourteen happy years
You shielded me from sorrow, cares, and fears;
Brought me the brightest buds, the fairest flowers
And mixed with gladness all my saddest hours.
Your age was double mine, they say, forsooth,
Who knew not how you kept the heart of youth,
And how your years at last seemed blest with mine
Until they were as one. The Life Divine
Is yours, my darling, now; oh, dropping tears!
Touch not the brightness of those happy years.

Fourteen happy years
We helped each other. You have wiped my tears,
And I kept yours from falling. We have felt
Our prayers mount up together as we knelt.
Together we have laid beneath the sod
Our dearest darlings; to the will of God
We have submitted, as we turned our eyes
Together, husband, to the self-same skies;
And, though your voice is silent in my ears,
I thank the Lord for Fourteen happy years.

Fourteen happy years
We walked together; when my footstep nears
The place where you went upward, shall I see
My husband stooping down to welcome me?

Oh! will you take me to your loving breast?
And bear me heavenward, when 't is time to rest?
Dear home, sweet home! you well may mourn his
    loss,
But I will dry my tears, and look across
Into the mansion that to us is given
For all the eternal years—Oh, Blessed Heaven!

MY NEW YEAR'S WISH.

TO C. S. W.

WHAT shall I wish for thee
    On this new Year,
Friend, whose bright face has often brought
    The sunshine here.

Shall it be wealth?
    Ah! that might be
A weight that dragged from Heaven to earth
    Continually.

Shall it be love?
    Ah! that is thine,—
The sweet earth love, so blest and true,
    And the Divine.

Shall it be fame?
    I do not know
Whether 't is good for thee and thine
    To have it so.

Shall it be power?
  Dost thou know how
To use it rightly every day and hour?
  I'll wish it now.

Let it be trust.
  Thine own and more,
A heart so full of heavenly peace, it must
  Be running o'er;

Be running o'er,
  Till thy brimmèd cup
Shall touch thy neighbor's heart, so void before,
  And fill it up.

This is my wish, dear friend,
  And, if 't is best,
I hope kind Heaven this priceless gift will send,
  And all the rest.

1883

HIS BIRTHDAY.*

WHAT birthday present could I send,
  This summer morn, to you, my friend?
What birthday gift would be in tune
With earth and heaven this day in June?

* Written for Mrs. Julia Stubbs on her husband's birthday.

His Birthday.

Shall I send flowers? A crimson rose
Upon the bush you planted, grows;
I pick it now, I kiss its face,
And send it to your dwelling-place.

Shall I send books? A volume waits
For you, of life this side the gates;
I press its leaves, so clean and fair,
And send it, darling, where you are.

Shall I send words of tenderness?
Or loving deed? or fond caress,
Such as you always gave to me
The birthday morns that used to be?

If I could all these tokens send
From earth to heaven, belovèd friend,
Would you look up with beaming eye
And thank me as in days gone by?

Ah, yes, your faithful love, I know,
Eternally will stronger grow,
And, though heaven's fulness be complete,
A gift from me would still be sweet.

They reckon not by natal days
Up there, a loving whisper says;
And it is so; but I am sure
Your love forever will endure.

Therefore, in this familiar place,
Made bright by your remembered face,
I can with your own soul commune,
And send my thoughts, through skies of June,
To you. My eyes to yours I lift,
My faithfulness, your birthday gift.

"GOD KNOWS WHY."

IN MEMORIAM—CARRIE BEATRICE COFFIN.

MY Darling! on the flash of lightning sped
    The news too quickly, "She you love is dead."
I hastened homeward as if you were there.
Only the lovely robe you used to wear;
Only a pure white form that held no more
Your blessed spirit, lay inside the door;
Only an angel face, whose close-shut eyes
Moved not, but seemed to look beyond the skies.
"Darling," I cried, "oh! wherefore must you die?"
A whisper seemed to answer, "God knows why."
Yes, God knows why, but to my feeble sight
'T is deepest darkness with no glimpse of light.
I miss you so at morning, noon, and eve,
And cannot think 't is wrong for me to grieve;
I miss you and I want you every hour;
The song has lost its sweetness, and the flower

Has lost its fragrance, and the evening prayer
Unanswered falls upon the pulseless air,
Because you join not, and I vainly try
To stop my tears, and whisper "God knows why."

He knows and sometime I shall surely know
The reason why, and yet the tear-drops flow
Unbidden, as your tenderness I miss,
And long, my darling, for your vanished kiss.
He knows, and some time I shall plainly hear
The blessed answer echoing in my ear;
Perhaps some danger lay along your road,
Some fearful trouble, or some heavy load
For you to bear; and so, my dear, I'll try
To murmur: "It is best, for God knows why."

FOUR YEARS AGO.

FOUR years! my darling, can it be
    That you have been away from me
So long? Yes, four New-Years have passed
Since I was happy. Oh! that last,
That happiest Christmas, when we sat
So glad, so gay, not knowing that
A shadow close beside us lay,
To darken every Christmas day;—
That happiest Christmas when you said
"I'm glad that we are here," and led
My tripping feet to find the path
Along December's aftermath.

Four years in heaven ! How much you know
That I know not ! Four years ago
We read the self-same books, and turned
The leaves together ; now, you 've learned
Heaven's mysteries. Why must I wait
Alone, confused, disconsolate,
And long to have your lips explain
The verses, one by one, again ?
Is it that I may better know
Heaven's alphabet before I go ?
Oh, then, dear Master ! wilt thou teach
My soul, to-day, the heavenly speech ?

"BE BRAVE."

"BE brave ! " she said,
    As I stood weeping by her dying bed,
And knew that long before the morrow's sun,
Too well my aching heart could tell "which one" ;
Knew she was slipping far beyond the touch
Of hand or lip that loved her, oh so much !
"Be brave, my own ! "
She murmured ; "oh, not long you 'll be alone ! "

And I have tried
To be so brave, since that sad day she died ;
Have tried to do the things she would have done,
And do them well ; but oh, from sun to sun,

The days are long, my song becomes a moan ;
No one to talk with, who is all my own !
I can't be brave,
When she who shielded, sleeps in yonder grave.

And yet, be brave !
It is not she who sleeps in yonder grave.
Heart ! Put on panoply of hope and trust ;
Eyes ! stop that weeping ; Trembling hands ! ye must
Take up her work ; Feet ! hasten ye to go
Wherever duty calls ; why falter so ?
I would be brave—
Dear Christ ! I fail without Thee ; come and save!

ONE YEAR AGO.*

ONE year ago, one little year !
   But oh, the weary miles
That lie between my dropping tears
   And those remembered smiles !
" One year ago this very day "
   They tell me—O'er my heart
A century has passed away,
   Since we have walked apart.

* Written for Mrs. Marcia Knapp one year after her husband's death.

Since we have walked apart, my own !
  Ah ! when I clasped your hand,
And felt your arm around me thrown,
  I could not understand
How desolate the path would grow,
  How hard the hills would be.
My darling ! One short year ago !
  And yet—so long to me ?

One year ago (ah ! can it be ?)
  I watched the coming train,
That brought my happiness to me,
  And did not watch in vain,—
The hurrying step, the opened door,
  The clasp, the jest, the kiss,
The loving smile, the cheery talk,
  A little heaven of bliss !

One year ago, one little year,
  Oh, sorrowing years to be !
Pass swiftly on, I 'll try to bear
  Whate'er ye bring to me ;
I 'll wait no more the coming train,
  With unavailing tears,
But look ahead, and look again.
  Come quick, immortal years !

"YOU WOULD NOT WISH HER BACK."

TO DR. H.

NOT wish her back?
    How can I help it? Everything I lack
When she is gone : she was my eye, my heart
My voice, my life, my soul's essential part,
My other self ; I saw all things through her ;
Heard through her ear, and if, perchance, there were
Some buds of beauty grew beneath my touch,
She sowed the seeds and made the colors such
As blossoms wish for. She has gone away,
But voiceless, lifeless, soulless, here I stay,
And deaf and dumb and blind I tread life's track,
How can I help it, if I wish her back?

She cannot come.
My wish is powerless ; let my lips be dumb.
Ungrateful lips ! Oh ! why forget to say :
"I thank thee, Lord, that for so long a way
She walked beside me ; that a life so sweet,
Its box of alabaster, at my feet
Poured out ; that for a little while
I lived beneath the sunlight of her smile ;
I am so glad, that, even for an hour,
Her holy influence held me in its power ;
I am so glad, and yet, dear Lord ! and yet"
Ungrateful lips ! oh : why do you forget?

HANGING THE PICTURES.*

DEAR pictured faces that look out
   From yonder sacred walls!
On those you loved, we cannot doubt
   Your benediction falls.

Oh, Father Venerable!† we
   Your simple faith recall;
Your all-embracing charity
   A lesson for us all.

Yes, we whose fathers you have blest
   Or joined in lasting bands,
Who felt upon our foreheads prest,
   Your consecrating hands,

Can almost see those shut lips move,
   And hear those accents quaint
Repeat the story of God's love—
   You were indeed a saint.

Oh, Pastor‡ of the young fresh heart
   That beat for us awhile,
The peace that loving doth impart
   Beams from that tender smile.

  * Read by the author at Farmington, Maine, 1893, on the presentation of pictures of the former pastors, to the Cong. Church, by Mrs. Julia W. Butler.
  † Rev. Isaac Rogers.
  ‡ Rev. Roland B. Howard.

We seem to hear your tuneful voice
   In message, or in song;
We listen, answer, weep, rejoice,
   Our faith and hope are strong.

We seem to take your friendly hand,
   We hear your questionings,
We answer, till you understand
   Our joys and sorrowings.

*   *   *   *   *   *

Glad spirits of our shepherds lost,
   If ye to-night can see
How we, on mountains tempest-tost,
   Remember, it must be

Ye will be glad; then, as we place
   These pictures here, we say:
Lord, may the influence, like the face,
   Hang over us alway.

"TILL DEATH DO PART."

"TILL death do part."
                   Say, will they cling,
These hands that now each other hold?
Cling close and firm through everything
   When life is young, when life is old?

Oh! answer truly.
　　　　　　　Like a prayer
Comes back the whisper of the heart:
" I will," floats up the morning air,
　" Till death do part."

FULFILMENT.

DO you remember, love, when we
　　Were side by side, you said to me
So often : " Darling, we will rest
Sometime, and then will see the west.
We 'll watch the waving wheat and ride
Together where the space is wide.
We 'll pick the roses of the south
Beyond the far Ohio's mouth,
And then, as in our youth, we 'll stand
Together on Kentucky's land
And see old friends who yet remain
And live the pleasant past again."

It is fulfilled, as we had planned.
I rest, I seek the wished-for land;
I look upon the prairie's green,
And watch the birds that fly between
Myself and you, but cannot say
　" Do you remember it this way?"
Into your ear.　I only see
The hills you loved to climb with me.

My hands alone the petals touch
That you would love to pick so much,
And all my being yearns anew
To talk it over, dear, with you.

Perhaps, how strange if it were so !
You think not of the fields below
But lost in wonder, stand and gaze
Forgetful of the parted ways.
Perhaps by tuneful banks you walk
And talk, or listen to the talk
Of lost ones found. Ah ! do you know
We dreamed of *this, too, long ago?*
The joyful resting, glorious scenes,
The meetings, greetings ? What this means
I know not, but it will be sweet
To talk it over when we meet.
I only know that God hath willed
This dream of ours shall be fulfilled.

MEMORY'S CLASS.

COMPANIONS of the distant days when life had touched its spring,
Across the years I reach to you as memories backward swing ;
I call your names ; stand side by side, and make a gray-haired row,
In that red schoolhouse where we went some forty years ago.

Speak for yourselves, companions, now, and as of
 old recite ;
What life's long term has taught each one, reveal to
 us to-night.
I am the teacher for an hour. Into your eyes I
 look,
And ask the questions from the leaves of time's
 old spelling-book.

I ask not for your secret thoughts ; my own are hid
 from you
(And yet the old friends read our hearts far better
 than the new) ;
I ask not for confession, dears, of every past mis-
 take ;
Tell me some bright experience for old acquaint-
 ance' sake.
Some blessed glimpses of the home and children
 nestled there,
Of one whose face for all the years has grown to
 you more fair ;
Of plans perfected, hopes fulfilled, of joys that still
 may be !
Companions of the olden days ! will you not give
 to me ?

As for myself, I have my griefs, and my besetting
 sins ;
I make great blunders ; all my outs are larger than
 my ins ;

My hope is strong, the path grows bright, and so, from day to day,
I think the Lord doth guide my steps into a better way.

I've had my doubts, I have them still; I am of self afraid;
I am too sensitive; I've mourned mistakes I never made.
But life is teaching many things, and here's my lesson now:
"Don't worry; God will make things right, and He alone knows how."

The lost and found are mingling here, the old beneath the new;
The manhood face, sometimes, and then, the child face peeping through;
The raven hair, the silver locks, the brown or rosy cheek,
The maiden's smile, the matron's frown, from past or present speak.

You at my side, so small and gray, so happy—or so sad,—
Has life brought any days to you like those your childhood had?
Have joys been yours? you bow your head? Ambitious? Ah! but few!
And work accomplished? Little? Then the foot is best for you.

And you, my blue-eyed merry mate, so songful and
    so sweet!
(Where are the roses that you wore when sitting in
    my seat?)
Has disappointment paled your cheek? And sorrow? Is this why
We miss, to-night, the starry light that sparkled in
    your eye?

And you, my golden-headed lad, who stood above
    the rest,
And still are rising! Have you had of life the very
    best?
The best you say? Love? Joy? Wealth? Fame?
    And do they yet remain?
Some things turn out just as they should. Stand
    at the head again.

And you, my serious, thoughtful child, so ready to
    begin,
So ready to give help, so mild, who cared not place
    to win,
So good, so kind, so laughing-eyed, with voice so
    sweet and clear,—
Tell me,—Alas! the gap is wide; she is not standing here.

She is not here; the space is wide, and many more
    I miss,
Who, all life's lessons here have learned, and
    changed Heaven's school for this.

We know not where ; we long to know, but we can
    only say,
They are not in the gray-haired row who 're stand-
    ing here to-day.

Oh, black-eyed, buxom, cheerful dame ! the twinkle
    of your smile
Reveals to me the very name you wore a little
    while.
Come and recite ! " Call up my boys ! " you answer ;
    bring them here !
For life has found its sweetest joys when children's
    steps draw near.

Class ! Come to order ! Toe the line ! Turn to the
    fiftieth page ;
Repeat in concert, word by word, the song of mid-
    dle age ;
Now close the book ; pass up the aisle. Gray
    heads ! ye may depart—
For memory must keep school awhile, in every
    scholar's heart.

OH, NO ! NOT OLD.

TO E. M. W.

AND are we old ?
    So nearly is life's little legend told ?
It seems, dear heart, as if 't were yesterday
That we were romping round the fields at play ;

It seems but yesterday that we could run
From early morning to the setting sun
And never weary. Tell me, can it be
That we are old ? It seems so strange to me.

Oh, no ! not old !
Though nearly threescore years have onward rolled,
The heart beats warmly as it beat of yore ;
Earth never was so beautiful before ;
And we can see it. Love is just as sweet
As when our mothers kissed us ;—yet 't is meet
That we should look whence we have come, and say,
" How many years have touched our heads to-day ?"

Oh, no ! not old !
Hearts may be young and all their freshness hold
When feet have lost their fleetness—when the eye
Must look through glasses for the starry sky ;
Hearts may be young, are young, when we can feel
Remembered pulses through our being steal ;
And so, I reach across the years and say,
It cannot be—we are not old to-day.

Not old ! not old !
Some years of life in labors manifold,
Some years of preparation, years of quest,
Of seeking, striving, finding what is best ;
Some years to learn the things we long to know ;
Some years to taste love's sweetness here below,
Before we reach the limit. Shall we then
Be old, dear heart, at threescore years and ten ?

Oh, no! not old!
Death is the birth of life to come.   Behold
A mystery : In God's own time we rise
New-born to Him, who hears His children's cries.
The years that have been, then, dear heart, shall be
As if they were not. This doth comfort me :
The nearer we approach that natal day,
The younger we may be—we 're young alway !

THE END.

www.ingramcontent.com/pod-product-compliance
Lightning Source LLC
Chambersburg PA
CBHW030355170426
43202CB00010B/1383